28-10-91

AD.

INSTITUTE OF MANAGEMENT AND LABOR RELATIONS SERIES—RUTGERS, THE STATE UNIVERSITY OF NEW JERSEY

Editor: James Chelius

1. *Reflections on the Transformation of Industrial Relations,* edited by James Chelius and James Dworkin. 1990

2. *Profit Sharing and Gain Sharing,* edited by Myron J. Roomkin. 1990

3. *The Mediator Revisited: Profile of a Profession, 1960s and 1985,* by Ruth F. Necheles-Jansyn. 1990

PROFIT SHARING
AND
GAIN SHARING

edited by
Myron J. Roomkin

Institute of Management and
Labor Relations Series, No. 2

IMLR Press/Rutgers University
and
The Scarecrow Press, Inc.
Metuchen, N.J., & London
1990

HD
2984
P76
1990

British Library Cataloguing-in-Publication data available

Library of Congress Cataloging-in-Publication Data

Profit sharing and gain sharing / edited by Myron J. Roomkin.
   p.   cm. — (Institute of Management and Labor Relations series ;
no. 2)
   Papers presented at a conference sponsored by the J.L. Kellogg
Graduate School of Management at Northwestern University and the
Profit Sharing Research Foundation, held in the fall of 1986.
   Includes bibliographical references and index.
   ISBN 0-8108-2335-7 (acid-free paper)
   1. Profit-sharing—United States—Congresses.   2. Gain sharing—
United States—Congresses.   I. Roomkin, Myron.   II. J.L. Kellogg
Graduate School of Management.   III. Profit-Sharing Research
Foundation.   IV. Series.
HD2984.P65   1990
331.2'164—dc20   90-8777

Dedicated to BERT L. METZGER, President (retired) of the Profit Sharing Research Foundation, for his commitment to the philosophy and practice of sharing in the employment relationship.

CONTENTS

Editor's Note   vii

Preface *(Myron J. Roomkin)*   ix

1. Participatory and Gain-sharing Systems: History
   and Hope *(George Strauss)*   1

2. Why Do Firms Adopt Profit Sharing? Evidence from
   Deferred Profit-sharing Plans *(Allen Cheadle)*   46

3. Labor-Management Relations: Unions View Profit
   Sharing *(John L. Zalusky)*   65

4. Employee Stock Ownership Plans: Consequences
   for Participation and Performance *(Raymond
   Russell, Patrick G. Grasso, and Terry J. Hanford)*   79

5. Labor-Management Relations: ESOPs in the Trucking
   Industry *(Grant M. Davis and Norman A. Weintraub)*   97

6. Gain Sharing and Profit Sharing as Strategic
   Considerations *(George T. Milkovich)*   109

7. Pay and Performance in Executive Compensation
   (W. Bruce Johnson)   123

8. Macroeconomic Implications of Pay and Perfor-
   mance: The Share Economy *(Martin C. Weitzman)*   137

9. Notes on Gain Sharing *(Robert J. Gordon)*   146

10. The Promise of Gain Sharing *(Robert B. McKersie)*   156

Notes on Contributors   167

Index   169

EDITOR'S NOTE

THE INSTITUTE OF MANAGEMENT AND LABOR RELATIONS of Rutgers University, The State University of New Jersey, was founded by the state legislature with a mandate to educate labor, management, and the public on matters concerning the employment relationship. With this series, it is our intention to further this goal by publishing books that will make a significant contribution to communicating the results of research on various aspects of industrial relations, human resource management, and employment policy.

JAMES CHELIUS
Series Editor
Institute of Management
    and Labor Relations
Rutgers University

PREFACE

LIKE FASHIONS, SOME PERSONNEL PRACTICES have a way of being rediscovered. Such has been the case with the idea of motivating employees by allowing them to share responsibility for the economic performance of the firm. Programs based upon this concept were first introduced as profit-sharing plans in the nineteenth century, repopularized during the Welfare Capitalism of the 1920s, and introduced again in the 1940s in a form called gain sharing, which provided an incentive to employees for contributing to increased productivity. In the 1970s, with the encouragement of the federal government, employee stock ownership became popular. However, nothing in the history of profit sharing, gain sharing, and employee stock ownership could have foretold the enormous enthusiasm in the 1980s for giving employees the economic incentive to participate in decision-making within the firm.

Behind this current popularity is a belief that shared responsibility and economic incentives can solve several significant problems facing American firms at this time. Such programs, it is claimed, can improve the competitiveness of America by improving the productivity of human resources, create greater responsibility for and pride in the quality of products, help control fixed labor costs, facilitate cooperative labor-management relations, and stimulate economic growth without inflation.

In the fall of 1986, a group of academicians and practitioners was brought together to exchange information and views on new developments in profit sharing, gain sharing, and related arrangements. The conference was sponsored by both the J.L. Kellogg Graduate School of Management at Northwestern University and the Profit Sharing Research Foundation, and it was supported by The Johnson Foundation of Racine, Wisconsin. All of the papers prepared for the conference appear as chapters in this book; three chapters have been added to round out the volume.

The first chapter, originally written by George Strauss as a background paper for the conference, serves as an introduction to the subject of shared responsibility. This comprehensive review of the literature looks at different types of programs within the broader context of all employee-participation arrangements. In theory, one weakness of employee-participation programs has been their failure to provide explicit financial payoffs to employees as a reward for their involvement in workplace decisions. Likewise, in the past some gain-sharing and profit-sharing programs—which represent such payoffs—have not fulfilled their potential because they failed to provide for adequate participation of workers in decision-making. Strauss concludes that gain sharing and employee participation have similar goals and can work together to build a more productive organization. However, formal programs of participation and performance rewards will not do the job if the organization lacks the commitment to make them work.

How can a firm create such commitment? Although Strauss does not look into the question, it would appear that the companies committed to performance sharing and employee involvement trace that commitment to a core philosophy of the organization and frequently the beliefs of a founding "father." Thus, performance compensation and involvement are not seen as programs to be appended to the activities of the personnel department, but rather are supported by the beliefs, values, and customs of the organization and are integrated with other human resources activities. This suggests that it is very difficult to simply transplant these practices successfully without first altering the culture of the organization—something not easily accomplished.

In reality, however, most companies are not deeply committed to performance-sharing compensation, even those that have it. Cheadle's paper on the characteristics of companies with profit sharing shows quite clearly that most firms with deferred profit-sharing plans (sometimes called savings plans) use these plans as *de facto* pension programs, not as instruments of employee motivation or performance.

Two chapters deal with aspects of performance compensation in unionized relations. In industries suffering from economic distress, employers have sought to reduce current wage costs and to base future compensation costs on economic performance and the ability of the company to pay. Gain sharing, profit sharing, and employee stock ownership appear to be particularly appropriate because they reward workers for demonstrated performance and do not permanently inflate base wages. Unions, for their part, understandably dislike the uncertainty of such approaches. These arguments, as John Zalusky indicates in his chapter, have led the labor movement to prefer employee stock ownership arrangements as a way of getting something back for concessions in collective bargaining. Norman Weintraub and Grant Davis show how one union, the Teamsters, has used the concept of employee stock ownership in the trucking industry in order to save jobs, union members, and trucking companies after the onslaught of deregulation.

Employee stock ownership plans have been receiving a great deal of attention because of the large number of leveraged buyouts and other financial manipulations in the news. Government has been especially interested in these plans because their very existence depends on the willingness of Congress to grant these plans special tax preferences. Accordingly, the General Accounting Office (GAO) undertook an exhaustive study of employee stock ownership plans in order to determine whether they affect the financial performance of companies and whether they give workers a greater say in the running of those companies. Russell, Grasso, and Hanford summarize the results of this investigation and conclude somewhat counterintuitively and disappointingly that employee stock ownership plans have their biggest consequence for the financial practices of companies and have little effect on the productivity or profitability of sponsoring firms. Moreover, these plans do little to increase the participation of employees in the governance of their companies. Admittedly, there is a body of literature that speaks more glowingly of employee stock ownership, and many firms are deeply committed to this concept for philosophical reasons. But, given the very controlled and careful methodology of the GAO's study, the burden of proof has passed to these proponents.

The issue of effectiveness is discussed further by Milkovich in Chapter 6. He reminds us that the effectiveness of an incentive compensation system must be judged in terms of its appropriateness under different situations. As yet, researchers cannot say when gain sharing or profit sharing are appropriate and when they are inappropriate. While he suggests some of the variables that might determine appropriateness, he also correctly calls for further theoretical and empirical research to clarify the proper contexts for these practices.

Johnson's chapter expands the scope of the discussion to include the compensation practices of executives. Ordinarily, profit sharing, gain sharing, and related programs are discussed as aspects of the compensation and participation systems of nonmanagerial employees. Yet, some of the biggest incentive compensation payments in the form of profit sharing are usually directed at managers, especially executives of large companies. This reality gives us the opportunity to observe, unencumbered by intraorganizational and hierarchical factors, how well incentive compensation packages can motivate behavior. In reviewing the literature on

the linkage between pay and performance for executives, Johnson
shows us that incentive compensation must be understood not just
from the strategic perspective, as Milkovich argues, but from the
perspective of shareholders, who structure compensation practices
for the purposes of monitoring and controlling the behavior of
managers.

In the chapters by Weitzman and Gordon the macroeconomic
perspective on gain sharing and profit sharing is discussed.
Weitzman's book, *The Share Economy,* did a great deal to popularize
the notion that incentive compensation, which might rise or fall
with the profits of the firm, could help the economy to create jobs
while fighting inflation. Legislators in England and the U.S. have
introduced legislation to make it easier for employers to initiate
such compensation plans. However, several economists, Gordon
among them, are unconvinced. The arguments against it are both
theoretical and historical

Finally, McKersie, who has been an active researcher on the
subject for many years, looks at the future of gain sharing.

Looking across these chapters, it is surprising that a few very
important questions were not examined in great depth. One of
these is the well-known issue of robustness: are these practices
resilient to economic downturns or other setbacks not caused by
the company or its employees per se? Second, although these
authors understandably focused on the necessary conditions for the
success of shared responsibility systems, the underlying theory of
why such programs should work at all is given less attention.

Perhaps the biggest issue still in need of clarification is why, in
this age of employee-participation schemes, employers are relatively resistant to compensation programs that give workers shared
responsibility for the performance of the organization. The answer,
I believe, goes beyond the belief that employees lack commitment.
Rather, the reluctance is due to the fact that such compensation
programs challenge traditional compensation practices that are at
the heart of bureaucratic personnel systems. These systems
developed because they served the efficiency needs of employers
and the security needs of employees, especially highly senior
employees. It will take a considerable amount of trust before both
sides abandon this comfortable tradition.

This collection of papers and the conference from which they
came involved the assistance of several people. Bert L. Metzger of
the Profit Sharing Research Foundation had the initial idea to bring
together teachers, researchers, and practitioners to exchange
information and views on profit and gain sharing. His assistance in
planning, organizing, and coordinating the conference helped to

make it a success. This volume is dedicated to Bert in recognition of his contributions to the promotion of gain-sharing and profit-sharing programs.

The generous financial support of The Johnson Foundation is also acknowledged. The findings and conclusions presented in these chapters are those of the authors and do not reflect the views of the foundation or carry its endorsement. William Boyd and Richard Kinch of the foundation were extremely helpful during the planning phases of this project.

I am also grateful to the authors of the papers. They showed more than the usual willingness to revise and update their manuscripts.

Leonie O'Donohoe helped by typing the manuscript, and Janet Weeks provided valued editorial services. I wish to thank them both.

MYRON J. ROOMKIN
Northwestern University
Evanston, Illinois

1. PARTICIPATORY AND GAIN–SHARING SYSTEMS: HISTORY AND HOPE

George Strauss

ONE OF THE DREAMS OF academicians and practitioners alike has been to satisfy simultaneously the desires of management for productivity, flexibility, and low cost as well as the desires of workers for higher incomes (and of some workers for creative, satisfying work). Participatory and gain-sharing systems—which, when combined, provide both pecuniary and non-pecuniary incentives—come as close as possible to making these dreams come true. Indeed, participation and gain sharing should reinforce each other.

Participation and gain sharing have both been very much in the news. Participatory schemes, such as job redesign and quality circles, are being widely adopted by nonunion firms; recently they have spread to the beleaguered unionized sector where they are often linked to concession bargaining. Meanwhile gain sharing is increasingly advocated both as an incentive for higher productivity and as a means for making labor costs more flexible. Profit sharing and employee stock ownership plans, in particular, have become more popular among both rich companies and those staving off bankruptcy.

Finally, among academicians and pundits the "share economy" is gaining considerable support as a solution for both inflation and unemployment.

The discussion below consists of three main sections. The first two deal with participation and gain sharing, respectively, and the last with combining the two techniques.

Participation

There is no generally accepted definition of *participation*. For our purposes, participation is a process which allows workers to increase their intellectual input into the work they do or to influence the conditions under which they work.

One can distinguish between two main forms of participation: *direct* and *representative*. With direct participation each worker makes a direct input into the decision process, as he or she does in autonomous work teams. With representative (or indirect) participation, the actual participants are representatives selected from the larger work force. Among the forms of representative participation are joint consultative committees (such as joint union–management safety committees) and worker representation on company boards of directors.

Another distinction can be made between *formal* and *informal* participation. Typical of informal participation is a boss–subordinate relationship in which the boss is receptive to every subordinate's suggestions. The stress in this paper will be on formal participatory schemes. Nevertheless, enough references to informal systems will be made to remind the reader that most participation occurs spontaneously, without formal organization. Also, quite arbitrarily I will exclude collective bargaining, though, in my opinion this is the most important form of participation there is.

A Brief History

In the 1920s the British Industrial Health Research Council's pioneering research (e.g., Wyatt and Langdon, 1933) showed that work could be made more meaningful in ways that would increase satisfaction, productivity, and quality. However, large-scale academic interest in participation dates from the famous Hawthorne-Western Electric Experiments.

Shortly afterwards a series of experiments by Lewin (e.g., 1953) and his disciples contributed to the belief that participatory groups were more productive than nonparticipatory ones and that decisions made participatively were more likely to be implemented than those made autocratically. Other work by the Likert (e.g., 1961) group at Michigan was consistent with these findings.

The 1970s brought widespread national concern with "blue collar blues," in part stimulated by a strike by young workers at a Lordstown G.M. plant that was attributed to the alienating conditions of assembly line work. Some observers noted a "revolt against work," particularly among younger, better-educated workers *(Work in America,* 1973, p. 186).

Although many observers believed that job satisfaction was rapidly declining, the evidence was unclear. It depended in part on whether one asked single, "facet-free" questions (such as "All in all, how satisfied would you say you are about your job?") or "facet-specific" questions regarding specific aspects of the job, such as pay, workload, or supervision. The vast majority (80+ percent) reported themselves satisfied on facet-free measures. By contrast, facet-specific measures indicated a steady drop in satisfaction through the 1960s and 1970s.

Meanwhile, highly influential studies by Hackman and Lawler (1971) found that some job characteristics (such as autonomy) were closely connected with both productivity and satisfaction. Thus, they concluded, job redesign might increase job satisfaction and raise productivity.

Even before this, a few progressive companies had begun to experiment with various forms of participation (Coch and French, 1948; Marrow, Bowers and Seashore, 1967). By the 1970s the terms *job enrichment* and *quality of worklife* (QWL) became popular, and experiments in workers' participation began to spread to mainline companies such as AT&T (Ford, 1969).

Aside from AT&T, much of the early experimentation was in "greenfield," nonunion plants, especially in the Southwest. Unions remained generally skeptical. By 1973, however, the national agreements negotiated by the U.A.W. and the major auto manufacturers contained provisions endorsing QWL programs, and joint committees were established to encourage and review them. A few auto plants experimented with QWL (Guest, 1979), but widespread adaptation of QWL programs in unionized plants had to wait until the recession of the early 1980s.

Significantly, the early experiments in unionized plants had as their ostensible purpose improving job satisfaction, working conditions, and product quality, with little mention of productivity. Only recently has productivity become an acceptable objective.

In the mid-1970s the Ford Foundation and the U.S. Department of Commerce helped finance a number of carefully monitored joint union-management QWL experiments. The three most fully documented of these occurred in Rushton, a coal mine in Pennsylvania (Goodman, 1979); Harman, an auto parts factory in Tennessee (Macy, 1982); and an engineering department at Tennessee Valley Authority (Macy, Peterson, and Norton, 1984).

Since 1980 formal participatory schemes have emerged from the experimental stage and have been increasingly adopted by industry. A 1985 survey conducted by the American Management Association found quality-circle type programs in 36 percent and autonomous work groups in 28 percent of the firms surveyed (AMA, 1985).*

---

*Reports of this sort are only suggestive since they indicate only whether a company has such a program *somewhere*. For example, a large, multi-plant company may have just one quality circle in one plant.

Why This Recent Popularity?

1. Economic pressures—such as the 1981 recession, increased foreign competition, and the impact of deregulation—convinced many managers and unions that almost heroic efforts were needed to cut costs, preserve jobs and prevent bankruptcy. Participatory schemes were viewed as a means of working together for mutual survival.

2. In the face of imminent job loss many unions agreed to substantial concessions in wages, fringes, and work rules. As a *quid pro quo* for these concessions, unions often insisted that management give them greater influence in determining organizational policies, often through the assignment of limited managerial responsibilities to joint committees, but also through stock ownership or even union representation on company boards of directors.

3. In some nonunion companies participation was viewed as a means of keeping unions out.

4. Interest in Japanese management is the current fad. Various forms of participation, especially Quality Circles, are seen as the secret of management success.

5. In an increasing number of cases participation may be required by a fast-changing technology. *Assembly-line* mass production work is being replaced by *custom* or craft technology (in which each job is different and general purpose machinery is used) and *process-continuous flow* technology (in which workers' primary function is to adjust or repair the equipment when it isn't working right.)* Both custom and continuous-flow technology require broadly trained workers who are committed to their work and prepared to exercise high orders of discretion (workers who, presumably, are more like the Japanese). Participation is particularly appropriate for these new technologies.

6. Finally, workers are changing too. They are better educated, and many have learned to expect and even demand opportunities for participation.

Perhaps the most important of the reasons for the spread of participation has been management's felt need to increase flexibility and reduce costs. Job enrichment and autonomous work groups, in particular, have been viewed as means of breaking down rigid job

---

*In an influential book, Piore and Sable (1984) suggest that we may be entering "The Second Industrial Divide," in which craft work will substitute for mass production technology.

classifications and work rules. Saving management money, rather than making workers happy, has been the main purpose of most recent change.

The Theory

There have been elaborate theoretical explanations of the virtues of participation (e.g., Lowin, 1968; Locke and Schweiger, 1979). More relevant to this paper are the reasons why participation *may* raise productivity and/or satisfaction, stressing that it doesn't always work this way.

1. Participation may result in better decisions. Workers often have information which higher management lacks. Further, participation permits a variety of different views to be aired. From this extensive discussion a higher quality solution may emerge. *On the other hand,* workers may be less informed than managers, and the premises upon which they make their decisions may be different.

2. People are more likely to implement decisions they have made themselves. Not only do they know better what is expected of them, but helping make a decision commits one to it (Staw and Ross, 1978). *On the other hand,* having made a decision, people become rigid. If decisions are made by groups, reaction to changing environments may be particularly slow.

3. The mere process of participation may satisfy such nonpecuniary needs as creativity, achievement, and social approval. *On the other hand,* not everyone has strong desires for creativity and achievement, or they satisfy these desires sufficiently off the job.

4. Participation may improve communication and cooperation; workers may coordinate with each other rather than requiring all communications to flow through management. *On the other hand,* participation is time consuming.

5. Participation tends to give people a sense of power. This reduces the need to show one's power through fighting management and restricting production. *On the other hand,* once people feel they have power they want to continue to exercise it. Once a precedent of participation is established, withdrawal of this "right" becomes difficult.

6. Participation frequently results in the setting of goals. There is considerable evidence that goal setting is an effective motivational technique.

7. Participation helps identify and train leaders.

8. If participation takes place in a group setting, a new element is added: group pressure to conform to adopted decisions.

Forms of Participation

Below I describe the major forms of participation (see Figure 1). For convenience I group these forms under three headings. *Job redesign* involves changes in the way jobs are done,* such as autonomous work groups. With *consultation,* workers make suggestions for change, but management's approval is required before they are implemented. *Consultation plus gain sharing* includes plans that are simultaneously both participative and gain-sharing techniques.

JOB REDESIGN

Job enlargement. This approach combines jobs "horizontally," typically lengthening the work cycle. At times workers may be given "whole tasks" and permitted to follow a job from beginning to end. Longer job cycles require additional skills and provide a greater sense of variety, task identity, and accomplishment.

Job enlargement may be associated with "broad banding," the combining of what were once separate job classifications. At the joint GM-Toyota plant in Fremont, California, all the unskilled job classifications have been combined into a single one. Changes like this one inspire some union critics of job redesign to call it workrule concession in fancy dress.

Job enrichment. This approach goes beyond job enlargement in that it adds "vertical" or quasi-managerial elements, especially planning, supply, and inspection. Thus it contributes to the workers' sense of autonomy and control over their work. For example, workers may control the speed of the machines they run and even turn these off for short periods; operators may maintain their own equipment; lab technicians may sign their own reports, rather than have bosses check them; maintenance people may decide priorities of repair tasks.

Autonomous work teams. Autonomous work teams are, in a sense, a group counterpart of job enlargement and job enrichment, in that employees are given wide discretion to organize their own work and to operate with very little supervision. Typically, these groups make their own work assignments and determine their own work routines, subject to overall workflow requirements.

---

*Not all forms of job redesign greatly increase participation. For example, job rotation is often viewed as a form of job redesign. However, it involves relatively little participation unless employees decide for themselves when they want to rotate.

Figure 1:
FORMS OF PARTICIPATION

JOB REDESIGN
> job enlargement
> job enrichment
> autonomous work teams

CONSULTATION
> suggestion systems
> quality circle and job involvement programs
> joint consultative committees
> membership on company boards of directors

CONSULTATION PLUS GAIN SHARING
> Scanlon Plan
> buyouts
> producers' cooperatives

Work teams have been given responsibility for developing relations with vendors, determining which operations can be handled individually and which by the group as a whole, setting work pace (perhaps fast in the morning and slow in the afternoon), training new employees, and, at one company, even keeping financial records.

Sometimes work-team members serve in roles normally reserved for staff personnel or supervisors: chairing the plant safety committee, redesigning work equipment, or troubleshooting customers' problems. At times the job of foreman is rotated among members of the group. When the new G.M. Saturn plant opens up, "councilors" (first-line supervisors) are to be elected by their workers. The Topeka Gaines dog food plant (once owned by General Foods and now by Quaker Oats) was set up with work teams of seven to fourteen members. Activities usually handled by separate groups—such as quality control, maintenance, janitorial work, and industrial engineering—became the responsibility of the group as a whole. Individual jobs were often rotated, but key decisions were made on a group basis. Initially, each worker was paid the same rate, with pay increases being given when the group decided that one of its members had picked up additional skills. The group screened new job applicants and apparently even "expelled" (discharged) poor performers.

The forms of participation just described involve changes in ongoing work organization. The next three—suggestion systems, quality circles, joint consultative committees and union membership on company boards of directors—permit workers (or their representatives) to suggest or recommend changes in work practices or conditions which management must approve before they are implemented.* By contrast, in autonomous work groups, workers can implement the changes themselves.

Suggestion systems. In the typical suggestion system a worker writes an idea on a special form which is evaluated by the suggestion director or a suggestion committee, usually in conjunction with the supervisor who might be affected. If a suggestion is accepted, the employee receives an award, often 10 to 25 percent of the first year's savings produced by the suggestion.

Not all suggestions increase productivity. A high percentage involve work environment rather than production techniques themselves. Their implementation may make work safer or more comfortable, or they may eliminate perceived inequities. In nonunion situations, suggestions may serve the same function as grievances in unionized situations. From a managerial point of view, among advantages of suggestion systems is that they highlight pockets of poor morale and expose poor supervision and violations of company policy.

Suggestion systems serve two main purposes: First, they give management the benefit of the employee's ideas on how to improve organizational efficiency. Second, they may increase job satisfaction and commitment through giving employees a chance to express their ideas, to display their creative talents, and to take pride in seeing their ideas accepted.

Quality circles and job involvement programs. Quality circles and job involvement programs (QC-JI) are the latest American fads and, in one form or another, have been widely adopted, often with considerable fanfare. The two programs are much alike. In some circumstances they operate much like autonomous work groups in

---

*I include union board membership as a form of consultation since unions typically constitute a minority of the membership and require approval of the management majority before their "suggestions" are implemented.

that workers can implement their own decisions. More frequently their function is akin to that of a group suggestion system.

QC-JI teams typically consist of small voluntary groups of workers from the same work area who meet together on a fairly regular basis to identify and solve quality and productivity problems. Sometimes their supervisor acts as their chair; other times it is a staff "facilitator" or even a union member. Frequently members of the group and the chair receive special training in such subjects as group dynamics and statistical analysis.

Despite their name, QCs often deal with subjects other than quality, for example work flow, productivity, safety, and workers' welfare generally. Often such committees start with housekeeping issues, and then, as their members gain confidence in working with each other, they progress to questions relating to quality and eventually productivity. In "operating teams," functioning in at least ten General Motors plants, workers have the responsibility for "inspection, materials handling, housekeeping, and repairs." They meet periodically "to discuss production problems, review the pay system, and discuss impending business decisions such as the introduction of new machinery or upcoming work schedules. . . . [T]he team regularly reviews the costs and revenues associated with the work area" (Kochan, Katz, and Mowrer, 1984).

Although instructed not to do so, at times QC-JI teams tread on areas normally reserved for collective bargaining and the grievance procedure. Understandably, supervisors and union leaders may well view them as potential threats.

Joint consultative committees. Since joint union-management consultative committees are *representative* committees which deal with issues involving more than a single workplace, they therefore differ from the shop-floor QC-JI committees, previously discussed. Joint committees were fairly common in American industry well before the concession-bargaining era, especially during wartime and recessions, periods when labor and management objectives appear more congruent (Jacoby, 1985).

Traditionally such committees dealt with matters that were considered peripheral to the main collective bargaining relationship (such as safety, training, and scrap reduction), matters about which the interests of the parties were seen to be sufficiently alike that they could be resolved in a cooperative, nonadversarial way. Like long-established Joint Consultative Committees in Britain (sometimes called "tea and toilet committees"), these American committees, which operated at both the company and plant levels, played rather minor roles.

Recently, joint committees have proliferated, especially in the automobile industry, and they have been given more important duties. Some deal primarily with personnel issues, such as child care or special chairs for people working on video terminals. Others, sometimes called steering committees, monitor and facilitate the development of QCs and job redesign at lower levels. (Union members of these committees, of course, sometimes view their role not as cooperative, but instead as insuring that joint activities don't violate workers' rights as guaranteed by the union contract.) Still others have been charged generally with reducing costs, improving productivity, and quality.

Recent auto contracts have spawned a maze of joint committees. One set of committees is charged with reviewing job design, new plant layout, changes in manufacturing equipment, and major new processes. There are plant-level committees (called "Mutual Growth Forums" at Ford) with the function of providing informal forums for exchange of information and the discussion of investment and other issues which might affect employment or workers' welfare. Another series of company-wide and plant-level committees administers the funds ($1 billion at GM) to provide training and new forms of employment for employees laid off due to technological change or outsourcing.* A joint union-management study group (including 60 union representatives) helped plan GM's new Saturn project to build subcompact cars (*Daily Labor Report,* December 21, 1983). At GM still other company-wide committees deal respectively with Health and Safety, Attendance, Substance Abuse Recovery, Tuition Assistance, and Skill Development and Training. Some of these committees administer substantial funds. Many have local counterparts, for example, a Hazardous Material Control Committee at each plant. Finally, to coordinate these various activities—and to reassure union activists who fear these committees will insufficiently protect workers' interests—G.M. has a capstone, overall Executive Board-Joint Activities Committee (*Daily Labor Report,* September 27, 1984).

Similar but less widely publicized committees exist in many nonunion companies. In only a few cases do these committees, whether nonunion or not, have independent powers or budgets (the joint GM-UAW training committee is very much an exception). For the most part these committees are advisory to management.

Membership on company boards of directors. Union repre-

---

*Technically it is inappropriate to label these last committees as merely "consultative" since they have operational responsibilities.

sentatives have been placed on the boards of Chrysler and American Motors, Pan American, Eastern and Western airlines, Wilson Foods, and several financially troubled steel and trucking firms. In addition there are worker directors (not always selected by the union) in a considerable number of ESOP and buyout situations, as described below.

Union leaders are troubled by the apparent conflict of interest that union board-member representation occasions. They are divided as to the extent to which they should take responsibility for making difficult production and investment decisions, some of which may involve layoffs. To date, this dilemma has been resolved in three ways: (1) the worker representatives are eminent outsiders who presumably are sympathetic to workers' interests but receive no specific instructions as to how to vote (this is the approach followed by the Teamsters union); (2) a key union representative is selected, but he or she resigns the union role (as did Robert Gould, former chief negotiator for Pan American pilots); or (3) a key union representative is selected, but he or she keeps away from the board when collective bargaining strategy is discussed (as did Auto Workers' President Douglas Fraser while on Chrysler's board). All three strategies are inconsistent with the common European view that the union-director's main role is to influence industrial relations decisions.

U.S. experience with union-selected directors is still too limited to generalize with confidence (but see Hammer and Stern, 1983). As has been the experience in other countries (Strauss, 1982), union directors in many cases have been handicapped by rules keeping board deliberations confidential, thus restricting them from communicating with constituents. Directors from the shop floor lack the technical expertise to make contributions in areas such as finance; by contrast, outside experts lack knowledge as to conditions within the company. Further, regardless of the union director's skill, management can usually keep key issues to workers off the board's agenda. In any case, boards, which meet as infrequently as once a quarter, may exert little real influence. Finally, worker directors are often unrepresentative of the rank-and-file and rarely communicate systematically with their rank-and-file constituents.

Despite these problems, Fraser reports that while on the Chrysler board he was able to stave off some plant shutdowns, and he vigorously opposed high salaries, bonuses, and substantial stock options for management while workers were still making concessions (Bokovoy and Cheadle, 1985).

CONSULTATION PLUS GAIN SHARING

Scanlon Plan. With an almost 50-year history, the Scanlon Plan is the oldest of the programs discussed here. Joining participation with gain sharing, the plan represents an effort to elicit worker ideas for increasing productivity by combining direct and indirect participation with financial incentives (its gain-sharing aspects will be discussed separately).

The typical plan provides for shop floor "production committees" (much like QC-JI committees) that meet periodically to discuss suggestions from individual employees and to formulate general plans for improving productivity. Rejected suggestions or suggestions that affect the plant as a whole are referred to plant-wide "screening committees," which include top management as well as union leadership. Savings due to increased productivity are shared by workers and company. Since bonuses are paid on a plant-wide basis, success of the plan depends heavily on the development of cooperative relationships among all the workers, line managers, and staff in the plant.

Note how the Scanlon Plan differs from the typical suggestion system. When the plan is successful, the following happens: Instead of individual rewards for accepted suggestions, the group as a whole gains whenever productivity is increased. The union takes an active part, instead of worrying whether suggestions will result in speed ups. Individuals cooperate with each other in developing suggestions instead of keeping ideas to themselves. Further, management suggests problems for mutual discussion, rather than waiting passively for suggestions.

The Scanlon Plan has been extensively researched (for summaries, see Lawler, 1977; Schuster, 1983; Driscoll, 1979; and Strauss, 1979). The evidence suggests that its success is heavily dependent on managerial and union *attitudes* as well as the ability of the two sides to make substantial changes in their patterns of *behavior.* Perhaps because cooperation is more difficult to achieve in larger organizations, plans are more common in small companies, though there is increasing experimentation with introducing them into individual plants of larger organizations.

Buyouts. A recent trend has been for workers to "buy out" distressed plants, rather than see them shut down altogether. One report documents 65 buyouts between 1971 and 1975 (Rosen, Klein, and Young, 1985), whereas another credits buyouts with saving 50,000 jobs in 60 plants *(Daily Labor Report,* July 18, 1983). The largest of these buyouts involved the 8,000-employee Weirton

Plant of National Steel and the 3,000-employee Rath Packing Company (the latter unsuccessful). More recently unions have threatened takeover and leveraged buyouts to protect themselves against unfriendly managements. This has occurred particularly in the airline industry (e.g., at Pan Am, Northwest and U.S. Air).

A number of buyouts during the mid-1970s occurred when conglomerates sought to shake off relatively unprofitable plants or plants in the wrong line of business. The more recent wave of buyouts involved more seriously troubled firms in immediate danger of closing. In these cases jobs were saved by a combination of worker equity contributions, bank loans, government loans and grants, benefit and wage cuts (as much as 30 percent of GM's former Hyatt-Clark plant), and partial layoffs. The appeal of such rescues is obvious. Companies find buyers for their worst operations rather than incur the costs and public blame for closing them. Most workers save their jobs, and unions get credit for helping them.

But changes in ownership often meant no (or very little) change in control, even though individual workers often received voting shares of stock and were occasionally elected to boards of directors. In fact, "buyout" arrangements were often put together with such haste that little thought was given to internal governance. Workers' prime motivation was to save their jobs, and radical new ideas might have scared off financial support. Indeed, bank loans and other financial assistance were often contingent on the retention of stable hierarchical management structures (Whyte et al., 1983). Until recently unions could offer little guidance in this strange situation. Currently, however, the Steelworkers union has developed policy guidelines for protecting workers' interests and has hired Lazard Freres to evaluate the feasibility of proposed buyouts.

Buyouts often appear quite successful at first: Profits improve, productivity climbs, turnover declines and apparently hopeless plants are restored to seeming prosperity. At least three factors may be at work: (1) wages and manpower are cut, thus increasing profits; (2) the newly independent plants are freed from the requirement to contribute toward corporate overhead; and, finally, (3) once the often formidable barriers to workers' ownership are overcome, workers feel a sense of triumph.

In many cases, after a year or so of worker ownership, disillusionment sets in. Workers move "from euphoria to aliena-tion" (Whyte et al., 1983). Once fear of job loss subsides, worker ownership, by itself, seems to have little impact on either productivity or satisfaction. For the average worker, the job and the boss are unchanged. Some companies are in too disadvantaged a position economically to be saved. Thus, despite substantial productivity increases under worker control and very large paycuts, the Rath Packing Company succumbed to an unfavorable economic environment (Hammer and Stern, 1986).

Producers' cooperatives. Producers' cooperatives can be distinguished from buyouts by the fact that they have been organized from the start to provide a high level of workers' control. Among the best known PCs are a series of plywood firms in the Pacific Northwest and several scavenger (garbage collection) firms in the San Francisco area. In addition, there are taxi PCs in some cities and a variety of largely counterculture "collectives." Of intense interest to worker participation buffs, PCs have been intensively studied (e.g., Jackall and Levin, 1984; Perry, 1978; Russell, 1985). However, they are inherently unstable and only a handful have survived more than five years as democratic organizations. (Some have been converted into more conventional businesses.)

Status Equalization

Before discussion of the problems associated with participation, it should be noted that some of the best-publicized participation experiments have been accompanied by important changes in status symbols. These have begun to reduce what a prominent union leader called:

> "the double standard that exists between workers and management. . . . Workers challenge the symbols of elitism typically taken for granted, such as salary payments versus hourly payment; time-clocks for blue-collar workers; well-decorated dining rooms for white-collar workers vs. plain, Spartan-like cafeterias for blue-collar workers; privileged parking for the elite but catch as you can for workers" [Bluestone, 1974, 47].

At the Gaines dog-food plant, for instance, there were no reserved parking lots, no time clocks, and no differentiation between management offices and worker lounges. Workers were free to make phone calls on company time (just like management). Many Japanese-owned plants in the U.S. require all employees, management and workers, to wear similar uniforms. Such reductions in status differentials not only tend to reduce dissatisfaction, but they also help develop an atmosphere of trust and confidence between workers and management and so reinforce the impact of participation.

Problems with Participation

While every form of participation has drawbacks of its own, there are a number of problems which plague participative schemes generally and thereby limit their application. The major ones are briefly discussed below.

Worker resistance. Not all workers want added responsibilities or enriched jobs; some would prefer their secure routines to remain unchanged. Some people already obtain all the challenge and stimulation they want, either at home or at work. Overstimulation can be even more frustrating than understimulation.

The evidence suggests that when jobs provide increased opportunity for learning and discretion, people with strong ego needs respond more positively than those with weak ego needs (Hackman, 1977). Culture and occupation make a difference too. Professionals trend to value participation more than nonprofessionals.

Of course, individual workers can be given the choice of working in redesigned or traditional jobs (and in a few companies the two forms of work exist side by side). Furthermore, various representative committees and consultative systems permit self-selection. Usually only a minority, often a small minority, engages in most of the participation. But this minority consists of those who are most anxious to participate and who probably have the most to offer.

Finally, workers may fear job loss, not an unreasonable fear since management's main purpose in introducing participation is to raise productivity and reduce labor costs. Workers are likely to engage in participation only if participation is associated with job security.

Management resistance. Participation is resisted and sometimes sabotaged by middle- and lower-level managers and especially by foremen (Klein, 1984; Bradley and Hill, 1983; Kochan, Katz, and Mowrer, 1984; Walton, 1980; Strauss and Sayles, 1980). For workers, one of the main advantages of participation is the greater freedom to make decisions on their own, rather than having managers hovering over them. Understandably this freedom is threatening to managers. Among the problems are the following:

1. Managers' *status* is threatened (loss of separate parking lots is symbolic of much wider losses).
2. Their *authority* is threatened. Workers are encouraged to make decisions on their own. They may even bypass supervisors and contact staff people and suppliers directly. Suggestion systems and QCs both threaten to reveal managers' mistakes.

3. In some cases, supervisors' very *jobs* are threatened. Job redesign may lead to one or more levels of management being eliminated.
4. Managers are forced to learn wholly *new techniques of supervision,* such as soliciting workers' ideas. Often these are completely at variance with what tradition has taught them is right. They are uncertain as to what they are supposed to do, and this is very threatening.
5. First-line supervisors feel *discriminated against.* They are forced to share power, but don't see their bosses sharing theirs. They are forced into a system that typically they had no part in designing. They see guaranteed job security for workers, but none for themselves.

Managers may resist unconsciously as well as consciously. Evidence suggests that the success of participation plans depends heavily on managers' trust in their subordinates and in their belief that their subordinates are in fact capable of making worthwhile suggestions (Ruh, Wallace, and Frost, 1973). Where trust is lacking (for example, where the supervisor views participation merely as a morale builder), the parties go through the motions of "counterfeit participation" (Heller, 1971), but the desired payoff in terms of productivity and satisfaction may not be obtained.

Union resistance. Adjustment is equally difficult for union leaders who are required to suspend their adversarial roles. Though unions overall have become somewhat more favorable toward participation over the last ten years, the transition has been painful. Unions find the problem of job dissatisfaction inherently difficult to resolve through the adversary techniques of collective bargaining. Noting that participative programs have been introduced into some militantly anti-union companies, many unionists still view these as chiefly union-busting techniques (Parker, 1985). They see them as forms of manipulation and speedup and as attempts to deflect workers' attention from their economic problems. As a unionist put it, "The best way to enrich the job is to enrich the pay." Finally, there is fear that such programs will "co-opt" workers and that unions will be diverted from their true mission.

Thus union attitudes are mixed. At the national level, the Auto Workers have been generally supportive (subject to appropriate controls). Another major union, the Machinists, has been generally hostile. In between are national unions which either (a) encourage local-level experimentation and provide staff support for such experiments, or (b) adopt a position of neutrality, allowing local unions to make their own decisions (Kochan, Katz, and Mowrer, 1984).

At the local level there is also considerable variation. A few locals actively resist all participative efforts. Others adopt a passive, "watch dog" policy, allowing management to introduce and administer various schemes as long as these don't interfere with the union's contractual rights. Still others take an active role and make participation a joint venture. To the author's knowledge, however, no union has taken the initiative to make shop-floor participation a contract demand.

Unionists object chiefly to job redesign programs that management introduces unilaterally, without consulting the union. But regardless of how such programs are introduced, they are likely to affect pay, promotional ladders, and job descriptions.

The thrust of collective bargaining in the U.S. has been to rigidify and codify personnel practices. In the typical unionized plant, decisions as to the allocation of work among workers are made on the basis of rigid, collectively bargained seniority and job description rules. Many workers believe strongly that job demarcation and seniority rules give them quasi-property rights in their jobs, rights which they are willing to fight hard to preserve.

Among the major causes of resistance to "concession contracts" in some plants is that they require giving up these long-enjoyed work rules. Job redesign combines some jobs and blurs the boundaries between others. Self-managing work teams tend to erase the sharp line between workers and managers, a distinction which American unions have long sought to maintain. New career patterns disturb established promotional ladders. Further, collective bargaining leads to what the Webbs called the "common rule"; by contrast, the whole participation movement promotes experimentation and diversity. Transition from one system to another is difficult.

Intergroup rivalries. Participation is typically introduced at an uneven rate in various parts of the organization. Nonparticipants frequently become jealous of the special privileges enjoyed by participants. This occurs even when the former are nonparticipants by choice.

Plateauing and atrophy. A common experience is that QC-JI goes through three stages. The first is one of overcoming suspicions and developing the skills to work together. Once this problem is solved, groups go through a second stage of relatively high activity. In the third stage interest begins to wane, the agenda of solvable problems grows smaller, and meetings become less frequent

(Walton, 1980; Griffin, 1988). Keeping QWL-JI programs going may be more difficult than getting them started. Without continuous effort, they may simply atrophy.

Plateauing is less of a problem with forms of job redesign than with QC-JI. With job redesign, duties are changed more or less permanently. Once employees learn to exercise autonomy (and management learns to permit it) the new responsibilities become internalized. But even the excitement of job redesign can peak. Once an enlarged job is learned, it too can become routine.

Management commitment likewise dwindles over time. In contrast with Japan and Sweden, where such programs have had strong support from engineering departments and line management, the support and responsibility for such programs in the U.S. is typically diffuse, with outside consultants rather than line management often being the prime movers (Cole, 1982). Participation is too often treated as a passing fad. Without continuing strong management support, shop floor programs are unlikely to survive. Indeed participation schemes need *champions,* high-level people with clout who really believe in participation.

Trust. For participation to work, a high degree of trust is required among all parties. Trust is frequently fragile. It can be easily dissipated if management lays off workers or pays itself big bonuses shortly after demanding wage concessions.

Pay. Pay is a problem throughout. As productivity and responsibilities increase, workers want more pay; they see themselves doing supervisors' work without supervisors' pay. Further, they think it unfair for management to keep all the benefits. Yet management often thinks psychic rewards should be enough and resists all forms of additional monetary compensation. Where compensation is increased, it is always a problem deciding how to distribute the increase. For example, if pay for lower-paid workers is adjusted upwards in multi-skilled work teams, the formerly higher-paid feel discriminated against.

As we shall see, gain-sharing plans are designed to mitigate these last problems.

Gain Sharing

Participation and gain sharing reinforce each other. In simple terms, participation provides a *method* whereby workers can increase production while gain sharing provides the *rewards* for so doing.

As the term will be used here, gain-sharing schemes are those designed to link economic rewards to performance according with some predetermined rules. Sometimes they are called "contingency based compensation."*

The current interest in gain sharing reflects a growing dissatisfaction with traditional compensation practices based on job classifications and seniority, adjusted by cost-of-living changes. It is argued that these systems are inflexible, especially in bad times; reward longevity rather than performance; and discourage teamwork and job switching. As a consequence there is an unparalleled amount of experimentation with alternative compensation schemes, especially with gain sharing (but also pay-for-knowledge and one-time bonuses).

In the sections which follow I will examine the most common arguments for gain sharing, describe five forms of gain sharing, and finally compare these forms in terms of their likely impacts on individual and organization effectiveness.

The Theory

In principle, gain sharing has a number of advantages.

1. Presumably people will work harder and more effectively if they receive economic rewards for doing so. Straight pay rewards one for showing up at work and doing the minimum amount of work not to get fired; gain sharing rewards efforts beyond that minimum. Economic rewards are particularly important motivational tools for those relatively uninterested in nonpecuniary incentives.

2. Beyond this, economic rewards have a nonpecuniary function. In a capitalistic society, they provide feedback: concrete evidence, both to oneself and to the larger society, that one's efforts have been successful.

3. Equity enters here, too. Employees feel it only fair that if they produce more then they should be paid more. They feel this particularly if the higher production is due to their own effort. But to a lesser extent they also feel they should share the organization's overall gains even if not due to their own effort. Thus, if

---

*I will also ignore gain-sharing plans available chiefly to executives, such as stock option plans. (But note that gain-sharing plans are more common for executives than for rank-and-file workers.)

management and stockholders get bonuses, so should they. (Whether workers are prepared to share in the organization's losses is another matter.)

This sense of equity may be disturbed if the method of calculation and distribution of rewards is viewed as inequitable; if, for example, a substantial increase in effort is rewarded by only a slight increase in pay.

4. Gain sharing arguably creates loyalty through paying over-the-market rates. Some economists might call it a "partial gift exchange" (Akerloff, 1982), a guarantee that workers won't "shirk." Further, some forms of gain-sharing payments, such as deferred profit-sharing plans, may reduce turnover. (However, since these benefits could be obtained just as well through paying above-market salaries or through defined-benefit pension plans, they are not unique advantages of gain-sharing plans.)

5. Gain sharing may develop a sense of commitment as well as a belief that employees and management share a common fate. Sense of commitment has a strong negative relationship to turnover (Mowday, Porter, and Steers, 1982).

Even if gain sharing doesn't lead directly to commitment, it may be what McKersie (See Chapter 10) calls "the frosting on the cake" on a human resources policy, which also includes high levels of job security and participation.

6. Gain sharing may make it easier for management to introduce new technology and work rule changes. To the extent economic benefits from these changes are shared, resistance might be lowered. (On the other hand, with some forms of gain sharing, such as piecework, these gains are often recaptured through retiming the altered jobs.)

7. As Weitzman argues in *The Share Economy,* by making part of earnings contingent on organizational performance, gain sharing makes labor costs more flexible and so reduces management's incentive to cut employment during downturns. In a recent empirical study, Cheadle (1987) suggests that wage flexibility is one of the main reasons why employers have shown so much recent interest in gain sharing. In any case, gain sharing may help justify paycuts.

8. Finally, compared to other forms of pay-for-performance, such as merit-rating, gain-sharing programs have one great advantage: they are based on objective rather than subjective criteria and so less likely to engender boss-subordinate hostility.

Types of Gain Sharing

PIECEWORK

Piecework or individual incentives represent perhaps the oldest and most common form of gain sharing.* Piecework rewards workers for their individual effort. By contrast, most other gain-sharing systems relate rewards to group or company-wide performance.

Piece rates can be set on the basis of either historical performance (average performance over the past) or time study. If based on historical performance, groups that worked hard in the past tend to be penalized compared with those who worked more slowly. Further, historical performance provides no guide when products or technology are changed. Thus most piece rates in manufacturing are set through time study.

In theory piecework makes every worker his or her own boss and thus considerably eases the supervisor's job. Most studies indicate a substantial (15-35 percent) increase in output after piecework is introduced. However, one of the earliest and best established findings of the young Human Relations field (later: Organizational Behavior) was that piecework had serious disadvantages. Though production jumps at first when piecework is introduced, it quickly stabilizes at a level which may be somewhat higher than the pre-piecework level, but below what might be produced if workers worked all out. Workers restrict production and exert strong informal pressure on "rate busters" who break the group-imposed "ceilings."

According to the classic studies, workers restrict production for a variety of reasons. Above all, they fear that, if they produce too much, management will retime their job and cut the rates. Even if management doesn't do this, they fear that if they work full out when they feel fresh, management will insist they work equally hard on other occasions when their energy levels are lower. Further, workers commonly believe (with justice) that there is a fixed amount of work to do. If some people work harder, others may be laid off.

But, as the classic studies vividly illustrate, this is not piecework's only drawback. Few jobs remain unchanged over time. Theoreti-

---

*Some people may exclude piecework from their definition of gain sharing. I discuss it here, in part because it provides a comparison with other forms of incentives.

cally, whenever a job is changed to make it either easier or harder
to do, it should be retimed. But time study is hardly an exact science
and its accuracy depends to a considerable extent on the
cooperation of the worker whose job is being timed. In practice,
time-study time often degenerates into a battle of wits between
time-study experts and workers, with workers usually winning.
Thus piecework rates tend to become "demoralized" over time, and
people do less work for the same amount of money.

There are other problems too. Regardless of how careful the
time-study, some jobs will be tighter than others (i.e., more work
will be required to meet the standard). This leads to squabbles
among workers over who will get the "richest" jobs. Further, it
creates tensions between workers on piecework and other workers
who bring them supplies or maintain their equipment, yet who do
not enjoy piecework. Additionally, since workers have a strong
incentive to put quantity over quality, piecework often requires
expensive quality control procedures.

Piecework is particularly unsuitable when either the product or
the technology is changing, or even when the market shifts,
resulting in long runs one month and short runs the next. It is also
inappropriate when quality standards are high and inspection
difficult. Perhaps because these conditions are becoming more
common, the percentage of manufacturing workers on piecework
in the U.S. appears to have steadily declined since World War II,
from 30 percent in 1947 to 18 percent in 1973-80 (Carlson, 1982).
Many organizations have decided that individual piecework is not
worth the candle and have either abandoned gain sharing altogether
or have moved on to other gain-sharing techniques such as those
discussed below.

GROUP INCENTIVES

With group incentives, each member of the group receives a
bonus based on the output of the group as a whole, instead of a
bonus based on his or her individual output. The "group" may
include an entire plant or company. More frequently it consists of
a single department or even an autonomous work group that works
on a single product or process. In these smaller groups, standards
are often set by time study, just as they are in individual piecework.

Group incentives are particularly useful when job assignments
(such as in steel mills) are so interrelated that it is difficult to
measure the contribution of any single employee to total production. Group incentives make it possible to reward workers who

provide essential services to production workers, yet who under ordinary piecework are usually paid only the regular day rates.

Group incentives encourage cooperation among employees, whereas individual piecework militates against cooperation. Since all members of the group share in the same bonus, conflict is reduced between workers on "tight" rates and workers on "loose rates." Rather than struggle with one another over choice work locations, materials, and job assignments—the sources of much friction under individual piecework—employees make their own allocation decisions, knowing that everyone will share in the final result. For example, waiters who pool tips are often anxious to help each other out of a jam.

On the other hand, group incentives share many of the disadvantages of individual plans. Even group piecework may require retiming when products are changed or new products introduced. Workers still fear that if they produce too much management will cut the rates. Also, since workers may feel that their individual efforts have little effect on the overall output of the group, they may be less motivated to work than under individual piecework. But since everyone's earnings are dependent on everyone's efforts, the group may pressure the laggard individual to work harder.

COST-SAVINGS PLANS

We come now to a set of incentives which are often called "gain-sharing plans." Given the broader meaning attached to "gain sharing" in this volume, I will call these plans cost-savings plans (CSPs). In each of these plans workers are paid a portion of the savings generated when costs fall below a predetermined level. Each plan can be implemented on a company, plant, or departmental basis. The three best known CSPs are Improshare, the Scanlon Plan, and the Rucker Plan. The main difference among them is in how these costs are calculated.

The **Improshare** plan is a group incentive. Like many forms of group incentive, it requires the calculation (usually through time study) of the standard hours which would be required under "normal" conditions to produce a unit of output. If the actual time required to produce any period's output is less than the standard hours allowed for this, workers and management share the savings, usually on a fifty-fifty basis. Thus, if it takes only 4,000 hours to put out 5,000 standard hours worth of output, the 1,000 hours saved are divided equally between management and workers. Each worker would earn a 12.5 percent bonus.

While Improshare plans have most of the advantages and disadvantages—including time study—of other forms of group incentive, the **Scanlon Plan** avoids time study. Although a variety of formulas are used, the most common one is based on the ratio of payroll to sales value of goods produced. The typical plan begins with a "normal" payroll-to-sales-value ratio—say, 40 percent. In a unionized situation this figure is determined through negotiations, although based generally on historical experience. If, in a given month, a group of workers with a "normal" ratio of 40 percent produces $100,000 worth of product, but do so with only $36,000 worth of labor, then there will a $4,000 savings ($40,000 "normal" payroll minus $36,000 actual). This, too, is divided among workers and management, often with 75 to 85 percent going to workers.

The Scanlon Plan eliminates the need to recalculate rates every time a new product is introduced. To the extent that wages move with the firm's prices, it also helps compensate for change in cost of living. However, it works best where the average labor intensity (that is, the "normal" ratio between payroll and sales value of goods produced) remains reasonably constant. When the product mix changes substantially or new technology is introduced the ratio may have to be renegotiated. The Scanlon Plan promotes quantity, not quality, and it provides no incentive to save materials.

The **Rucker Plan** formula is much like that of the Scanlon Plan, except it is based not on the value of total production but on value added. Since value added is calculated by subtracting the cost of raw materials (and services procured outside the company), it provides an incentive to save materials.

As we have seen earlier, the Scanlon Plan is normally tied in with an elaborate network of participative committees. While the Improshare and Rucker plans might also be associated with such committees, the participative element is less frequently emphasized.

Under all three plans bonuses are typically paid out on a monthly basis, usually as a percentage of pay. Rapid feedback about performance is usually stressed.

PROFIT SHARING

Profit-sharing (PS) plans provide employees with a bonus which is normally based on some percentage of the company profits, or profits beyond some fixed minimum.

Compared with previously discussed forms of gain sharing, PS eliminates the need to recalculate the benefit formula whenever technology, product mix, or prices change. Further, it reduces the sense of inequity which may occur if the company makes big profits and workers get nothing. Through allowing employees to share in the fortunes of the company as a whole, it is designed to make them feel like partners.

PS is of particular interest today because of its role in what has been called the "Share Economy," to be discussed later, as well as its important role in the 1986 steel and telephone negotiations.

PS plans come in many different forms. Perhaps the most important distinctions involve whether:

(a) the bonus is paid directly to employees as earned (cash plans) or is deferred until some later date. Some plans involve a combination of both, with employees often being given some choice as to how their bonus is to be paid.
(b) the amount of the bonus is determined by a relatively fixed formula (say, 10 percent of all profits in excess of 5 percent of net worth) or is discretionary and can be varied from year to year.
(c) the plan is an addition to a traditional pension plan or takes its place.

Each of these distinctions will be discussed below. But first a bit of background.

PS has had a long history and has been tied in with early efforts at employer paternalism. The Procter & Gamble plan dates back to 1887. Early plans were most widely introduced in production processes where piece-work was inappropriate because the product was nonstandardized and quality of great importance. Most early plans were cash.

PS's rapid growth dates to World War II, when deferred plans were exempted from wage controls on the grounds they were noninflationary. Since that time, deferred plans have been more popular than cash ones, in part because deferred plans offered employees substantial tax advantages.

By 1984 there were approximately 360,000 companies with approved deferred or combination plans in the U.S. These covered 20 million employees. Assets of PS funds came to $175 billion, no small amount (Profit Sharing Research Foundation, n.d.). In addition, according to other estimates, there were 100,000 to 150,000 cash plans. Together perhaps 20 to 25 percent of the private-sector workforce is covered by one form of plan or another (Cheadle, 1987).

The majority of plans have been introduced in nonunion companies; unions have been generally suspicious of them.

Nevertheless, PS has played an important part in recent concession bargaining. Among the firms agreeing to share profits in return for wage concessions were Ford, GM, Weyerhaeuser, and Caterpillar Tractor as well as a number of steel and telephone companies. The 1986 Inland steel contract, for example, provides that workers will receive 10 percent of the firm's operating earnings plus a "gain-sharing" bonus that rewards workers for improved quality and productivity.

Plan characteristics. Only limited data are available as to the whole population of U.S. PS plans. However, Hewitt Associates, in cooperation with the Profit Sharing Council, annually collects data about the Council's membership. Selected data from the 1984 survey are presented in Figure 2 (see page 27). These data (based on reports from 529 companies employing 1.7 million workers) are generally quite consistent with those from previous years. However, they should not be taken as representative of PS plans generally, but only of "leading" firms that have a sufficient interest in the subject to join the Council.

In 1984 employer contributions by Hewitt companies averaged 8.8 percent of pay. Indeed the range of payments for the nine-year period, 1976–1984, a period of rapidly fluctuating profits, was from 9.9 to 8.8 percent, suggesting that employer contributions are relatively constant, regardless of profits. A somewhat larger sample, collected by the U.S. Chamber of Commerce for the period 1965-84, shows that PS payments moved within the narrow range of 1.0 to 1.2 percent of payroll, except for two years, 1978 and 1979, when it was 1.4 percent (Chamber of Commerce, various years).

Cash or deferred? The vast majority of the Hewitt plans (82 percent) were deferred. Only 3 percent were pure cash, while the remainder combined cash and deferred payments. Even so, enough plans included a cash option so that, of the Hewitt companies' total 1984 employer contributions of $1.3 billion, $300 million was in cash.

Deferred plans are more common in small companies (perhaps, as we discuss below, because they often serve as substitutes for pension plans). Almost all of the plans arising from concession bargaining—such as at Ford, GM, and in the steel industry—are purely cash.

While cash plans are easier for employees to understand there may be serious morale problems in profit-less years if no bonuses are paid. Deferred plans have longer survival rates than cash plans, perhaps because with deferred plans the morale-sapping impacts of profit-less years are felt less directly.

Figure 2:
Characteristics of 529 Selected Profit-Sharing Plans

Form of profit-sharing plan (number of plans)	All plans	>5000 participants
Cash		
Also offering pension plans	9	0
Not offering pension plans	5	0
Total	14	0
Deferred		
Also offering pension plans	104	17
Not offering pension plans	328	9
Total	432	26
Combined		
Also offering pension plans	36	6
Not offering pension plans	47	3
Total	83	9
Method of determining employee contribution (percentage of plans)		
Specific formula	17.9%	60.0%
Discretionary	42.0	11.4
Percentage of employees' pay or deposits	17.1	8.6
Combination and other	20.0	12.5
Average employer contribution		
(as a percentage of pay)	8.8%	6.2%
(as a percentage of profits)	24.1%	12.0%

Source: 1985 Profit Sharing Survey, 1984 Experience, conducted by Hewitt Associates in cooperation with the Profit Sharing Council of America, 1985.

Fixed or discretionary? In order to qualify for tax benefits prior to 1956 a firm's contribution to a PS plan had to be computed according to a prearranged formula which related profits to benefits. Many firms objected that fixed formulas caused serious employee morale problems since profits, and therefore annual contributions, fluctuated so widely. To meet these objections a 1956 Treasury ruling permitted tax-qualified plans with "discretionary" (i.e., no) formulas, as long as contributions were "substantial and recurring" and somehow based on profits. Some companies, for example, make a minimum annual contribution to the fund, even in years of low or negative profits.

As Figure 2 indicates, only 17.9 percent of the 1984 Hewitt sample based their bonuses entirely on a specific percentage of profits. Indeed, 17.1 percent were based not on the rate of profits but purely on participants' pay or contributions—and so were really thrift rather than PS plans. Drawing on broader data, Cheadle (1987) estimates that "from 20–50 percent of existing profit-sharing plans" are discretionary.

On the other hand, as with deferred plans, the discretionary plans are concentrated in the smaller organizations. In 60 percent of the Hewitt plans with 5,000 or more participants, the bonus was based on a fixed percentage of profits.

Psychological research suggests that the motivational impact of any incentive system is a function of the degree to which performance is perceived to be tied to reward. With both discretionary and deferred plans the relationship between effort and reward is uncertain and so the motivational impact is diluted.

As a substitute for pensions? At least in smaller companies, deferred plans often serve as substitutes for pension plans. Of the 432 purely deferred plans in the 1984 Hewitt study, 78 percent were offered by companies without a pension plan. Cheadle (1987) finds that firms that offer one kind of plan are less likely to offer the other. Firms that offer both sorts tend to be the larger ones.

By establishing a PS rather than a pension plan, the employer can bypass ERISA's pension-plan red tape. Further, it avoids making a rigid and costly commitment which might be difficult to meet during bad years. Additionally, if the plan is discretionary, the employer can provide a fairly steady flow of income into the employees' retirement fund but do so on a purely voluntary basis. This flexibility is especially attractive to small employers.

Adding to the impression that many so-called PS plans are really pensions or savings plans, some companies encourage employee contributions to the fund and even match these contributions. Indeed it is common for employers to switch from one form of benefit plan to another, especially (prior to the 1986 tax-reform legislation) from PS to 401(k) deferred compensation plans in which employers match at least part of their employees' contributions. Potentially, PS provides less retirement security than do pension plans, especially those with defined benefits. How well do they do in practice? A study by the Profit Sharing Research Foundation found that the benefits paid by 27 out of 33 large PS plans provided retirement which exceeded the "typical pension standard" (defined by 1.3 percent of final average pay times years of service).

Despite company efforts to provide stable contributions, compared with defined-benefit pensions, PS is a rather risky way of earning retirement benefits. To reduce this risk PS funds may be invested in a variety of financial vehicles (with employees often given some choice as to how their account is to be handled). Occasionally PS funds are invested in the employer's own stock. However, this occurred in only 19 percent of the Hewitt survey's plans and in only 3 percent of the cases were the plans allowed to invest more than half their assets in this stock. To further reduce the risk, some companies use PS contributions to buy their employees the equivalent of insurance company annuities.

Some drawbacks. As do other forms of gain sharing, PS plans suffer from a number of drawbacks.

1. An employee's reward has only a tenuous relationship to his or her own contributions. Many of the factors contributing to profit are not under workers' control, either individually or as a group. It is easy to think of situations, where despite workers' increased efforts, profits drop, perhaps because of a soft market or foreign exchange losses. Only in a relatively stable market are profits likely to be closely linked to productivity.

2. Deferred plans relate pensions to company earnings years ago rather than employees' needs today, thus further weakening the effort-reward relationship.

3. Morale may plummet if profits drop, especially when workers have exchanged wage cuts for PS. General Motors workers were quite dissatisfied when they received no profit-sharing bonus in 1986 when both Ford workers and GM managers received substantial ones.

4. Profit sharing, particularly discretionary plans, switches risks to employees which might otherwise be borne by management. Two types of risk are involved: (a) that profits and therefore employer contributions to the PS fund will fluctuate, and (b) that the value of the fund itself will fluctuate over the years, especially if the fund is invested in the employer's own stock. Employers may reduce the first risk by making minimum payments to the fund regardless of profits. The second risk may be reduced by investing the fund conservatively.

Research findings as to PS success. According to several studies PS firms outperformed nonsharing firms on a number of dimensions: profits as a percentage of net worth *and* of revenue; growth in sales, net worth, dividend rate, and market prices of stock; and productivity (Metzger and Colleti, 1971; Metzger, 1978; Howard, 1979; Kruse, 1988). Left undetermined is the direction of causation. Do PS companies perform better *because* they have PS or are exceptionally successful companies—those already performing better—more likely to share their good fortune with their employees? A relevant piece of evidence: Kruse (1988) concludes that the adoption of profit sharing is associated with a 2.5-4.2 percent increase in productivity. In other words, after companies adopt profit sharing their productivity increases faster than does that of comparable companies which do not adopt profit sharing.

More than most companies, PS firms tend not to have profitless years (Cheadle, 1987). This may be due to the motivational aspects of the plan itself. Alternatively, only companies which already have assured profit flows are likely to adopt PS. In any case risky companies appear less likely to introduce PS.

The Weitzman plan. Martin Weitzman's *The Share Economy* has excited interest and controversy among economists and policy-makers throughout the world. Since it is discussed at length elsewhere in this volume (see Chapter 8), I will cover it only briefly.

Weitzman argues that wage rigidity is one of the basic causes of both unemployment and inflation. In times of recession, wages remain stable and employment is cut. In times of prosperity wages may move up, but because of a ratchet effect, never drop back down again.

The solution, he argues, is to divide employee compensation into two parts, first a fixed wage (say $10 an hour), and secondly a share in the profits (let us assume $5 an hour, under normal conditions and less when business is bad). According to economic theory, an employer will hire additional workers if the added cost of each additional worker is less than the added revenue that this worker will produce. If the fixed labor cost is $10 an hour, an employer will hire more workers than if it is $15. True, hiring more workers may reduce each worker's share of profit (and hence his or her compensation) but the company's total profit will increase.

If fixed wages are set low enough, the share economy would presumably have three beneficial effects.

1. There would be an excess demand for labor, thus reducing unemployment and providing companies an incentive to train the unskilled. Any shock to the economy (say an oil price

increase) will be automatically translated into pay cuts rather than unemployment.

2. Since total compensation per worker declines (at least in the short run) as employment expands, prices will be held in check.
3. The "positive externalities of a tight labor market" will encourage risky investment and foster economic growth. A virtuous circle of expanding output and demand will ensue. Real income will rise and eventually this will more than make up for any short-term losses in compensation.

In support of Weitzman's plan, a recent study finds that profit-sharing manufacturing firms have "smaller employment decreases than other manufacturing firms: when the unemployment rate increases by one point, non-profit sharing firms have a 3.0% decrease in employment, while profit-sharing firms with all employees participating have only a 2% decrease" (Kruse, 1988, iii). Although there is a possibility that firms that adopt profit sharing are also more likely to adopt other "progressive" personnel policies, such as avoiding layoffs, one small study suggests that this is not the case (Finseth, 1988).

Six major objections have been raised to the plan.

1. Employers and, especially, unions will resist its introduction. While the working class as an aggregate (including those presently unemployed) might gain from the plan, the immediate impact on currently employed workers will be a paycut. Even if forced to accept profit sharing, workers might seek to restrict employment growth. Further, even partial basing of wages on profits conflicts with the union goal of equal wages for equal work. Weitzman would overcome all this opposition through the tax system. (Indeed, the 1986 bargaining round suggests that under proper conditions unions may accept profit sharing as a substitute for wages.) In any case, Weitzman assumes that workers will have little say in determining the level of employment. Thus his approach is philosophically inconsistent with worker participation.
2. The plan assumes that if compensation per worker is cut, companies can and will cut prices significantly. But labor cost may be only a small part of total cost. Prices may be set via oligopoly and managers may fear that a price cut will set off competitive retaliation.

The plan also assumes that it will be easy to sell the additional output that an additional worker may produce. But this may not be the case. The market may be relatively inelastic to price cuts, especially in the short run. Further, the technology may be fixed in the short run, preventing added useful employment.

3. In a dynamic share economy some firms' profits may go up while others' may go down, often quite rapidly. When this happens interfirm differences in employees' compensation would fluctuate equally rapidly. Under conditions of full-employment, employees would quickly move to firms offering higher total compensation. Such rapid shifts in the labor force could waste firm-specific training and harm the economy's overall efficiency.

4. There is a substantial recent labor economics literature which seeks to explain why wages are so stable, even in the non-union sector. It argues that workers are risk-adverse and enter into "implicit contracts" with their employers so as to avoid wage fluctuations. If so, both parties would have a considerable incentive to manipulate reported profits to make them seem more stable. Even today there is a great deal of manipulation of this sort.

   On the other hand, American workers' apparent preference for *earnings* stability (as opposed to employment stability) may be an artifact of our culture (or our post-war industrial relations system). Japanese workers, it is claimed, have learned to prefer employment stability. American workers might do likewise.

5. According to efficiency wage theory, firms pay more than the market-clearing wage for a variety of reasons: to reduce turnover, to recruit better workers, to prevent workers from shirking (because otherwise they might lose a good job) and to induce loyalty and commitment through receiving a "gift." Compensation cutting would eliminate these advantages, even if the compensation cuts consisted exclusively of reduced profit-sharing bonuses. But without cuts in current employees' compensation no new employees would be hired (Levine, 1987).

6. Profit sharing, by definition, decreases management's share of profits. Thus, investment activity may decline (Estrin et al., 1987). If the going rate of interest is 12 percent, an investment with a 15 percent total return might not be made if management keeps only 10 percent. On the other hand, profit sharing may encourage debt financing.

STOCK OWNERSHIP

From some points of view worker stock ownership is the ultimate form of incentive. Stock ownership presumably motivates workers through giving them a sense of identity with the company. Being owners, it is hoped, they will be more committed and so work harder and more effectively. Their incentive will be to increase not just profits but the company's underlying worth.

Stock ownership plans have been given considerable credit for the highly publicized success of a number of firms noted for their productive workforce. A much debated question, to be considered below, is whether the success of companies such as this is due to stock ownership itself or to other forms of unorthodox managerial techniques these companies practice.

Especially because of tax reasons, most stock ownership plans today take the legal form of an "Employee Stock Ownership Plan" (ESOP). An ESOP is a trust established to receive stock from the employer (or cash to purchase stock from existing owners) for distribution to individual accounts of participating workers. The allocation of stock is based typically on relative compensation, but other formulas are also used, including credit for seniority.

As workers accumulate seniority, they gradually acquire vested rights to the stock in their accounts. In general, however, workers receive financial benefits only after they retire or sever employment. In publicly owned companies (that is, stock listed on the stock exchange) employees must be able to vote their shares. Three quarters of ESOP firms are privately held, however, and here workers' voting rights are often restricted.

Exact figures are difficult to come by, but there were an estimated 8,777 ESOPs in 1987 covering some 8,860,000 workers *(Employee Ownership Report,* 1988). In 1983 ESOPs and stock bonus plans held total assets of $19 billion with a median value of $5,226 per worker (U.S. General Accounting Office, 1986).

Why have ESOPs spread so rapidly? Aside from the widespread belief that ESOPs increase worker motivation and commitment, there are at least four reasons.

1. *Tax provisions.* A series of changes in the tax laws, beginning in 1974 and continuing through the 1986 tax reform, provided strong financial incentives for firms to adopt ESOPs. A firm's ESOP contributions, for example, are tax deductible.
2. *As fringe benefits.* As with profit-sharing plans, ESOPs are fairly frequently adopted as substitutes for pension plans,

especially by companies that argue that they can't afford the fixed financial commitment that pensions require.

3. *To retain control.* ESOPs have been used increasingly to shield companies from hostile takeover offers or as a means by which effective control of a closely controlled firm can be passed from one generation to another without requiring company stock to be sold to pay estate taxes. ESOPs have also facilitated leveraged buyouts.

4. *Concession bargaining.* As a part of concession bargaining in depressed plants, unionized workers have fairly frequently agreed to wage cuts in return for promises to share in future profits or in stock, the latter typically in the form of ESOPs. One of the more dramatic cases involved Chrysler, which was required to contribute $165 million worth of company stock to an ESOP as a condition for a government $1.5 billion loan guarantee. In 1984 Chrysler employees owned 16 percent of its stock, with the typical holding being worth $4,500 *(Daily Labor Report,* July 10, 1984). ESOPs are also common in the financially troubled airline industry, where employees received 13 percent of Pan American, 25 percent of Eastern and Republic, 33 percent of Western, and substantial portions of the stock of smaller airlines.* Similar stock-for-wages trades have also been common in trucking and steel firms.

Union attitudes. Unionists have traditionally been antagonistic to worker stock ownership and to the principle of worker ownership generally. They argued that worker ownership gave workers the illusion of ownership without any real control and that it was chiefly a management technique to make unions unnecessary or to cut wages. They have been particularly opposed to replacing pension plans with ESOPs.

Faced with the prospect of substantial job losses, however, many unions changed their position. Wage cuts combined with stock ownership are better than cuts with nothing at all. Today, when companies plead poverty, unions increasingly respond, "If you can't give us money, give us stock." Stock ownership, some unions now

---

*According to one calculation, the workers at Chrysler gained more from the increase in the value of their stock than they gave up in wage concessions (Rothschild-Whitt, 1985). At Western, PSA, and Republic Airlines, each of which was bought up by a larger airline, workers made at least as much money by selling their stock as they had lost earlier through concession. *(Employee Ownership Report,* 1987, p. 6.)

argue, is a legitimate union objective, provided it is in addition to decent wages and fringe benefits.

Potential problems. ESOPs have been subject to considerable criticism. First, it is argued that they are inadequate substitutes for pension plans. The payoff to the worker is distant in time and uncertain, being dependent on the price of the stock. This places workers' retirement security at considerable risk since there are no guarantees that company stock will have any future value. Further it requires workers to put "all their eggs in one basket." If the company fails, employees may lose both their jobs and their retirement income.

Secondly, numerous abuses have been reported, especially the use of employee-owned stock to support management in takeover and proxy fights, under circumstances when independent stock-holders might have preferred to sell their shares or vote for a new management.

Finally, as mentioned above, workers often have limited say in how their stock is voted. In only a small minority of cases do they sit on the company board (or on the ESOP's board of trustees). Even in these cases the worker-directors are usually handpicked by management and are not expected to play an active role (Hammer and Stern, 1983). The few exceptions have occurred in "buyout" situations (discussed above).

Research findings as to ESOPs' success. Studies of the impacts of ESOP plans have proliferated almost as fast as the plans themselves (for reviews, see Tannenbaum, 1983; Kruse, 1984, 1988; U.S. General Accounting Office, 1987). The results are mixed. According to some studies ESOP firms have been more profitable than comparable non-ESOP firms (Conte and Tannen-baum, 1978; Blasi, 1988), more productive (Marsh and McAllister, 1981), increased employment faster (Rosen and Klein, 1981; Trachman, 1985; *Employee Ownership,* 1986), enjoyed higher sales growth, net operating margin, book value per share, and return to equity (Wagner, 1983). Other studies as to company performance are less encouraging. Thus Tannenbaum, Cook, and Lohmann (1984) found no significant difference between ESOP and conventional companies in profits, productivity and technological adaptiveness.

Research to date has still not determined whether ESOP firms become more prosperous as a result of employee ownership, or whether prosperous firms are more likely to establish ESOPs to begin with. Quarrey (1986) compared the performance of ESOP companies before and after they adopted ESOP, finding that these companies grew more rapidly after adopting ESOPs when compared both with their pre-ESOP growth and a matched sample of non-ESOP companies. On the other hand, an elaborate study conducted by the U.S. General Accounting Office (1987) found no direct relationship between the adoption of ESOPs and either productivity or profitability. Neither profitability nor productivity was related to other variables such as type of industry or percent of stock owned by the ESOP, with one important exception: ESOP firms had significantly higher production levels than non-ESOP firms when "nonmanagerial employees, acting through work groups or committees, make managerial decisions, either on their own or acting with management" (p. 28).

It is still not clear, however, how much of any improved performance is due to ESOP's adoption and how much to other managerial changes made at the same time, although Kruse (1988) argues that such managerial changes are small. One conclusion seems reasonably safe, however: Ownership and participation do more to raise productivity than does ownership standing alone (U.S. General Accounting Office, 1987; Quarrey, 1986; Cable and Fitzroy, 1980; Jones, 1982).

The numerous studies of attitudinal and behavioral change under ESOPs report mixed results. Some conclude that such factors as motivation, job satisfaction, perceived worker influence and organizational commitment have improved; others find no significant differences (for summaries, see Tannenbaum, 1983 and Kruse, 1984). According to perhaps the most extensive of these studies (covering workers in 37 diverse ESOP firms) satisfaction and commitment are significantly influenced by (a) the size of the company's contribution to ESOP (the amount of stock the participants receive), and (b) management's philosophical commitment to worker ownership (Rosen, Klein, and Young, 1985). Whether the ESOP owned a large percentage of the company's stock, whether the stock carried voting rights, and the reasons why the ESOP was established in the first place did not affect worker attitudes.

Evaluating Forms of Gain Sharing

As we have seen, each gain-sharing plan has its strengths and weaknesses. Perhaps we can evaluate them by comparing them against an ideal plan.

An ideal plan might have the following characteristics, some of which are difficult to obtain simultaneously: (1) there would be a direct relationship between individuals' contributions and their economic rewards; (2) employees always would be rewarded for actions under their control and never penalized for developments outside their control; (3) individual identification and commitment to organizational objectives would be fostered; (4) group pressures would be mobilized to support organizational objectives; (5) rewards would be paid off rapidly; (6) administration would be easy; (7) the plan would seem equitable; (8) it would be easily understood; (9) the stream of rewards would be relatively constant and riskless; and (10) the level of compensation would meet market tests.

Gain-sharing plans may be ranged on a continuum starting with individual piecework and running through group piecework, cost-saving plans, profit sharing to ESOPS. This continuum is based both upon the number of workers who divide the reward and on the number of factors upon which the reward is based. For convenience we shall call plans on the individual-incentive side of the continuum *narrow plans* and those at the other end *broad plans*.

Contribution-reward relationship. The ideal plan would link economic rewards directly to the employee's own contributions to organizational success. "Contributions" could include not just quantity of output, but also such factors as quality, reduction in scrap loss, suggestions for greater efficiency and willingness to adjust to technological and other change.

The larger the number of workers who divide a reward, the weaker the linkage between the individual's contributions and his or her own rewards. Individual piecework provides the strongest incentives for quantity of output. Group piecework may motivate greater cooperation between individuals, but the incentive for individual effort is diluted. Still broader forms of gain sharing may divide the reward among so many people that the individual contribution-reward relationship (or incentive) becomes minimal.

Rewarding appropriate behavior. An ideal plan would always reward people for actions under their control and never penalize them for developments outside their control. Unfortunately no form of gain sharing comes close to passing this test. Individual pieceworkers, for example, are rewarded for quantity rather than quality, although both are under their control. On the other hand, their earnings may be penalized by poor maintenance support. At the other extreme, the efforts of an individual ESOP member may have virtually no effect on stock prices, but he or she may be easily penalized for events elsewhere the world.

Group pressures. If a work group supports such organizational objectives as higher production and quality, it may apply crude or subtle pressures on those who fail to cooperate. But such group pressures may not be felt beyond the face-to-face level. Scanlon Plan experience suggests that individual departments often success-fully pressure their *own* members, but if one department starts blaming another for bottlenecks leading to lower bonuses, the second department may reject the blame and pass the buck. Thus group pressures are less likely to be successful in broader forms of gain sharing and broad gain sharing may engender bitterness rather than cooperation.

Piecework may have negative effects. Its individual form may divide groups while the group form may accentuate divisions between departments. Further, piecework often creates an adver-sarial relationship between workers and management.

Commitment. Gain sharing may *help* build commitment to the unit (group, plant, or company) on which the plan is based; however, as emphasized below, it is not likely to do this in the absence of other organizational policies, such as job security and opportunities for participation.

Though this commitment is often a weaker incentive than the money awards provided by narrower plans, highly committed workers identify with their units' success and so are prepared to work for its goals. Further, committed workers are less likely to quit and more likely to accept or implement changes.

Quick payoffs. Motivational theory suggests that rewards are more effective if they follow quickly after effort. This is particularly the case where rewards provide feedback as to the success of one's efforts. Individual and group piecework pass this test, as do most cost-saving plans. But even cash profit-sharing plans pay out only annually, while the rewards from ESOPs or deferred profit-sharing plans may not be enjoyed for years.

Easy administration. Piecework plans are expensive to design and maintain, especially when they are based on time-study. As technology changes it is becoming increasingly difficult to identify and measure individual performance, particularly on an objective basis. Broader plans are based on more objective measures and easier to administer.

Perceived equity. Satisfaction with rewards is a function not just of the reward's size but also of whether workers feel the reward system is fair. Time-study is often felt to be inequitable. But sophisticated workers may likewise suspect that profit figures and stock market prices may be manipulated.

The credibility of a plan depends in part on the trust that workers have in their management. There is a good deal of evidence that participatively set pay schemes are felt to be fairer and in general tend to be more effective (Lawler, 1977).

Easy to understand. In all cases simplicity should improve the credibility and image of gain sharing plans. Some piecework formulas are extremely complex, but the same can be said of some cost-saving, profit-sharing, and employee-stock ownership plans.

Constant, riskless rewards. Among the main thrusts of U.S. industrial relations has been to transfer the economic risks of life from employees to their employers. Health and medical insurance, sick leave, seniority, and pensions are all evidence of this trend. And, as mentioned in regard to the Weitzman plan, many economists now view steady wages as another form of risk shifting. Certainly it is widely believed that workers have a strong preference for a steady, predictable income flow.

All forms of gain sharing increase the riskiness and variability of employees' income. Individual and group piecework earnings may drop as workers are moved from "loose" to "tight" jobs. Scanlon Plan bonuses depend on product mix. Profits and stock prices fluctuate continuously and in ways hard to predict. Nevertheless the broader forms of gain sharing may be more risky (or at least have greater subjective probability of risk) than narrower ones. After all, workers understand what makes piecework earnings fluctuate. They find the stockmarket less predictable.

If workers must depend for their retirement income on deferred forms of gain sharing, their insecurity is increased considerably. If these funds are invested in the stock market, they risk large losses. If they are invested in the employer's own stock and the employer goes out of business, the employee may lose both job and retirement income. As mentioned earlier, unions and managements may exaggerate the extent to which workers are risk adverse (some love betting on races), and these attitudes might be changed. Change may be slow, however, and risk is one of gain sharing's weak points.

Meeting market tests. A gain-sharing system will fail if unit labor costs become so high that the organization's products become uncompetitive or if individual compensation falls so low as to cause strikes or make it difficult to recruit new employees. These problems are more likely to occur with piecework than with profit sharing or ESOPs.

The current focus in the U.S. is on broader gain-sharing plans. Older forms of piecework are being abandoned. (AT&T finally eliminated its historic manufacturing incentive system in the 1986 contract, but had to pay its workers to do so.) The narrower systems provided stronger incentives, but just for production. As technology changes, individual productivity is becoming harder to measure and other factors are becoming more important. As Lawler (1984) puts it, the broader systems produce:

> "a much less direct connection between individual perform-
> ance and reward, and therefore a less powerful motivator than
> are individual piece-rate incentives. Clearly then, there is a loss
> here in comparison to piece-rate incentive plans, but the
> expectation is that the loss will be made up" [p. 19].

To the extent that the loss is made up, it is through the development of identification, commitment, and a more cooperative "organization climate." But gain sharing alone is unlikely to engender cooperation. Among other requirements are job security and various forms of formal and informal participation.

Conclusion: The Relationship Between Participation and Gain Sharing

Participation schemes and broader forms of gain sharing reinforce each other, but only when these are consistent with managerial policies and practices generally.

By itself participation provides important nonpecuniary rewards, but in a money-oriented society these rarely are enough. Narrow gain-sharing plans (such as piecework) provide strong direct incentives but suffer from the limitations we have just discussed. Broader gain-sharing schemes, on the other hand, lack piecework's direct incentive power. Instead, when combined with participation, the broader plans serve three functions. First, they provide feedback as to the success of joint, participative efforts, thus showing symbolic (as much as monetary) recognition for these efforts. Second, the fact that management shares gains with the workers legitimates the demands which management makes on them.* And, third, gain sharing points out that everyone is part of one organization. In short, such successful gain-sharing plans foster a sense of commitment and cooperative involvement (or organizational culture). In economists' terms, they strengthen the internal labor market.

Cooperative attitudes are fragile, however, and can be easily destroyed if they are inconsistent with management practice.

---

*It is important that management and workers share both losses and gains, that when concessions are called for there be equality of sacrifice. This is something which some large organizations ignored when they granted their officers large bonuses shortly after having won concessions from their union.

Indeed the participative and gain-sharing systems discussed here are merely formulas. Some never come to life. Others have only a few months of accomplishment before plateauing, after which apathy sets in. The sad fact is that most participative committees merely go through the motions. Few broad gain-sharing schemes affect either productivity or attitudes—certainly not alone.

For example, three of the participation plans we examined—the Scanlon Plan, buyouts, and producers' cooperatives—also involve gain sharing. Yet the success of the Scanlon Plan requires more than an occasional committee meeting; it requires radical changes in both management and union attitudes and behavior. Similarly, though buyouts and producers' cooperatives are formally worker-owned companies, their chances for success or even survival are considerably limited unless formal worker ownership is accompanied by considerable actual worker control.

To be more specific, for formal participation and gain sharing to be successful, formal participation needs to be heavily supplemented with informal participation, including a good deal of communications upwards and down. Both power and status differences need to be reduced. As mentioned earlier, even symbolic changes, such as the elimination of special management parking lots and dining areas may make an important difference. Above all, substantial job security needs to be provided.

Participative and gain-sharing systems can be used to foster the development of the more basic attitudes mentioned above. For example, both systems can be introduced cooperatively, rather than being imposed from the top. Quarterly profit-sharing reports can be used for general discussions as to where the organization is going and as a springboard for goal setting and cooperative planning efforts. Once this occurs, profitless months may have less serious impact on morale.

Unfortunately for the success of these systems, they are being adopted at a time when American industry is being torn between two strategies. On the one hand, there is considerable interest in the development of "high commitment" organizations in which broadly trained employees identify with the organization and are prepared and trusted to exercise high orders of discretion. Along with this comes a commitment from the firm to provide job security for its employees and the opportunity to develop a satisfying career (not just a job). Participation and gain sharing play an important role in such a high-investment-in-human-capital strategy.

Conversely, many organizations are in turmoil. The economy is shifting from manufacturing to service. Many previously stable industrial giants (e.g., AT&T) are being forced to "restructure" and "downsize," sometimes as a result of leveraged buyouts and the like. Quite often such organizations have a desperate need for cashflow. As a consequence they liquidate their human assets at a rapid rate. Not only are skilled workers, professionals, and managers thrown on the ash heap, but expensively nurtured "corporate cultures" are quickly shattered. Participation and gain sharing under these circumstances have little meaning.

To conclude, formal participation and broad gain sharing are partial means to the end of developing a more committed, cooperative workforce. But they are unlikely to be successful if the larger environment is unfavorable.

References

Akerlof, G.A. "Gift Exchange and Efficiency Wage Theory: Four Views." *American Economic Review* 74 (1984): 79–83.

American Management Association. *The Changing American Workplace: Work Alternatives in the 80's.* New York: American Management Association, 1985.

Blasi, J. *Employee Ownership: Revolution or Ripoff?* Cambridge, MA: Ballinger, 1988.

Bokovy, P., and A. Cheadle. "Interview with Douglas Fraser." *Labor Center Reporter* 137. Institute of Industrial Relations, University of California at Berkeley (January 1985): 2.

Cable, J., and F. Fitzroy. "Cooperation and Productivity: Some Evidence from West German Experience." *Economic and Social Democracy* 14 (1980): 163–80.

Carlson, N.W. "Time Rates Tighten Their Grip on Manufacturing Industries." *Monthly Labor Review* (May 1982): 15–22.

Cheadle, A. "The Incidence of Profit Sharing Plans: An Economic Explanation." Unpublished Ph.D. dissertation. University of California at Berkeley, 1987.

Coch, L., and J.R.P. French. "Overcoming Resistance to Change." *Human Relations* 1 (1948): 512–532.

Cole, R. "Diffusion of Participatory Work Structures in Japan, Sweden, and the United States." In Paul Goodman, ed. *Change in Organizations.* San Francisco, CA: Jossey-Bass, 1982.

Conte, M., and A. Tannenbaum. "Employee Owned Companies: Is the Difference Measurable?" *Monthly Labor Review* 101 (July 1978): 22–28.

Driscoll, J. "Working Creatively with the Union: Lesson from the Scanlon Plan." *Organizational Dynamics* 8 (1979): 61–80.

Employee Ownership Report 6 (May 1986): 1.

Employee Ownership Report 7 (January 1987): 7.

Employee Ownership Report 8 (September 1988): 1.

Estrin, S.; P. Grout; and S. Wadhwani. "Profit Sharing and Employee Share Ownership." *Economic Policy* (April 1987): 13–57.

Finseth, E. *The Employment Behavior of Profit-sharing Firms: An Empirical Test of the Weitzman Theory.* Unpublished senior thesis, Harvard University, 1988.

Ford, R.N. *Motivation Through Work Itself.* New York: American Management Association, 1969.

Goodman, P. *Assessing Organizational Change: The Rushton Quality of Work Experiment.* New York: Wiley, 1979.

Griffin, R. "Consequences of Quality Circles in an Industrial Setting: A Longitudinal Assessment." *Academy of Management Journal* 41 (1988): 338–58.

Guest, R. "Quality of Worklife—Learning from Tarrytown." *Harvard Business Review* 57 (July 1979): 76–87.

Hackman, R.J., and E. Lawler. "Employee Reaction to Job Characteristics." *Journal of Applied Psychology Monograph* 55 (1971): 259–286.

Hammer, T., and R. Stern. "Worker Representation on Company Boards of Directors: Effective Worker Representation?" *Proceeding of the 43rd Annual Meeting of the Academy of Management.* August 1983, 364–368.

Hammer, T., and R. Stern. "A Yo-Yo Model of Cooperation: Union Participation in Management at the Rath Packing Company." *Industrial and Labor Relations Review* 39 (1986): 337–349.

Jackall, R., and H.M. Levin. *Worker Cooperatives in America.* Berkeley: University of California Press, 1984.

Jacoby, S.M. "Union Management Cooperation in the United States During the Second World War." In M. Dubofsky, ed. *Technological Change and Workers' Movement.* Beverly Hills, CA: Sage, 1985.

Jones, D. "British Producer Cooperatives, 1948–68: Productivity and Organization Structure." In Derek Jones and Jan Svejnar, eds. *Participatory and Self-Managed Firms.* Lexington, MA: Lexington Books, 1982.

Klein, J. "Why Supervisors Resist Employee Involvement." *Harvard Business Review* 84 (September 1984): 87–95.

Kochan, T.; H. Katz; and N. Mower. *Worker Participation and American Unions.* Kalamazoo, MI: Upjohn Foundation, 1984.

Kruse, D. *Employee Ownership and Employee Attitudes.* Norwood, PA: Norwood Press, 1984.

———. *Essays on Profit-sharing and Unemployment.* Unpublished Ph.D. dissertation, Harvard University, 1988.

Lawler, E. "Pay for Performance: A Motivational Analysis." Los Angeles: Center for Effective Performance, University of Southern California, 1984, mimeo.

———. "Reward Systems." In J. Richard Hackman and J. Lloyd Suttle, eds. *Improving Life at Work.* Santa Monica, CA: Goodyear, 1977.

Levine, D. "Efficiency Wages in Weitzman's Share Economy." *Economic Letter* 23 (1987): 245–49.

Lewin, K. "Studies in Group Decisions." In Dorwin Cartwright and Alvin Zander, eds. *Group Dynamics.* Evanston, IL: Harper, 1953.

Likert, R. *New Patterns of Management.* New York: McGraw-Hill, 1961.

Locke, E., and D.M. Schweiger. "Participation in Decision-Making: One More Look." In Barry Staw and L.L. Cummings, eds. *Research in Organizational Behavior,* Vol. 1, 1978.

Lowin, A. "Participative Decision-Making: A Model, Literature Critique, and Prescriptions for Research." *Organizational Behavior and Human Performance* 3 (1968): 68–106.

Macy, B. "The Bolivar Quality of Worklife Program: Success or Failure?" In Robert Zagar and Michael P. Rosow, eds. *The Innovative Organization.* New York: Pergamon Press, 1982.

Marrow, A.J.; D.G. Bowers; and S.E. Seashore, *Management by Participation.* New York: Harper and Row, 1967.

Marsh, T.R., and D.E. McAllister. "ESOP Tables: A Survey of Companies with Employee Stock Ownership Plans." *Journal of Corporation Law* 6 (Spring 1981): 551–623.

Metzger, B.L. *Profit Sharing in 39 Large Companies.* Evanston, IL: Profit Sharing Research Foundation, 1979.

Parker, M. *Inside the Circle: A Union Guide to QWL.* Boston: South End Press, 1985.

Perry, S. *San Francisco Scavengers.* Berkeley: University of California Press, 1978.

Piore, M., and C. Sable. *The Second Industrial Divide.* New York: Basic Books, 1984.

Profit Sharing Research Foundation. *Profit Sharing: Philosophy, Practice, Benefit to Society.* Evanston, IL: n.d.

Quarrey, M. *Employee Ownership and Corporate Performance.* Oakland, CA: National Center for Employee Ownership, 1986.

Rosen, C.; K. Klein; and K. Young. *Employee Ownership in America.* Lexington, MA: Lexington Books, 1985.

Rothschild-Whitt, J. "Who Will Benefit from ESOPs?" *Labor Research Review* 1 (Spring 1985): 71–82.

Ruh, R.; R. Wallace; and C. Frost. "Management Attitudes and the Scanlon Plan." *Industrial Relations* 12 (1973): 282–288.

Russell, R. *Sharing Ownership at the Workplace.* Albany: State University of New York Press, 1985.

Schuster, M. "The Impact of Union-Management Cooperation on Productivity and Employment." *Industrial and Labor Relations Review* 36 (April 1983a): 415–430.

———. "Forty Years of Scanlon Plan Research." In Colin Crouch and Frank Heller, eds. *International Yearbook of Organizational Democracy* 1 (1983b): 53–72.

Staw, B., and J. Ross. "Commitment to a Policy Decision: A Multi-Theoretical Perspective." *Administrative Science Quarterly* 23 (1978): 40–64.

Strauss, G. "Quality of Worklife and Participation as Bargaining Issues." In Hervey Juris and Myron Roomkin, eds. *The Shrinking Perimeter: Unionism and Labor Relations in the Manufacturing Sector.* Lexington, MA: Lexington Books, 1979.

Strauss, G., and L. Sayles. *Personnel,* 4th ed. Englewood Cliffs, NJ: Prentice-Hall, 1980.

Tannenbaum, A. "Employee-Owned Companies." *Research in Organizational Behavior* 5 (1983): 235–268.

Tannenbaum, A.; H. Cook; and J. Lohmann. "The Relationship of Employee Ownership to the Technological Adaptiveness and Performance of Companies." Unpublished paper, Ann Arbor, MI: Institute for Social Research, 1984.

Trachman, M. *Employee Ownership and Corporate Growth in High Technology Companies.* Washington, DC: National Center for Employee Ownership, 1985.

U.S. General Accounting Office. *Employee Stock Ownership Plans: Interim Report on a Survey and Related Economic Trends.* Washington, DC: U.S. General Accounting Office, 1987.

———. *Employee Stock Ownership Plans: Little Evidence of Effects on Corporate Performance,* Washington, DC: U.S. General Accounting Office, 1987.

Wagner, I. "Report to the New York Stock Exchange on the Performance of Publicly Traded Companies with Employee Ownership Plans," cited in Carey Rosen, Katherine Klein and Karen Young. *Employee Ownership in America.* Lexington, MA: Lexington Books, 1985.

Walton, R. "Establishing and Maintaining High Commitment Work Systems." In J.R. Kimberly and Robert H. Miles, eds. *The Organizational Life Cycle.* San Francisco, CA: Jossey-Bass, 1980.

Whyte, W.F.; T. Hammer; C. Meek; R. Nelson; and R. Stern. *Worker Participation and Ownership.* Ithaca, NY: ILR Press, 1983.

Work in America. Cambridge, MA: MIT Press, 1973.

Wyatt, S., and J.N. Langdon. *Fatigue and Boredom in Repetitive Work.* Industrial Health Research Council, Reprint No. 77, Great Britain, 1933.

Zwerdling, D. "Employee Ownership: How Well Is It Working?" *Working Papers for a New Society* 7 (1979): 15–27.

———. *Democracy at Work.* New York: Harper, 1980.

2. WHY DO FIRMS ADOPT PROFIT SHARING? EVIDENCE FROM DEFERRED PROFIT-SHARING PLANS

Allen Cheadle

THERE IS GROWING INTEREST in profit-sharing arrangements among a number of influential groups, including academics, the business community, and policymakers. At the same time there is currently no reliable empirical evidence indicating what the impact of various policies might be or how profit sharing will evolve in the absence of policy initiatives.

There have been a number of studies examining profit sharing and employee stock ownership plans—why they are adopted and their impact on worker morale and productivity (see, for example, Conte and Tannenbaum, 1977; Stern and Hammer, 1978; Stern et al., 1979; Long, 1981; Rhodes and Steers, 1981; Stern and Tove, 1981)—but they have focused on wholly employee-owned firms or firms where profit-sharing payments are a significant part of total compensation. The majority of profit-sharing activity, measured by the number of workers covered, occurs in firms where the profit share or stock distribution is a small fraction of total compensation. Since the expansion of profit-sharing activity, if it occurs, will involve its greater use by all firms in all sectors of the economy, an investigation into factors influencing the development of profit sharing should examine why all firms, including "marginal" profit-sharing ones, adopt plans.

The research reported here examines the critical factors influencing a firm's decision to adopt profit sharing. The focus is on the use of deferred profit sharing in large firms, the most significant subgroup in terms of the number of workers covered (Metzger, 1964). In deferred plans, profit shares are paid into a trust, deducted as a current business expense by the firm, but eligible for withdrawal by the employee only upon separation from the firm. In cash plans, profit shares are distributed directly to employees, either quarterly or annually. Since most of the current interest is in cash profit sharing (Weitzman, 1984), it is hoped that the issues related to the choice between deferred profit sharing and other fixed methods of deferred payment will be relevant for the choice between cash profit sharing and fixed hourly wages and salaries.

The standard reasons given for adopting profit sharing (incentives, flexibility) provide only a limited explanation for the observed patterns of (deferred) profit-sharing activity. A more convincing explanation is that deferred profit sharing is a "pension substitute" adopted to provide a predictable source of deferred income, and that observed variation in its use can be attributed to the length of experience with pensions in the particular industry and/or region. Locations with a longer history of pension plans are more likely to use pensions and less likely to use profit sharing as the primary source of deferred income.

New Data Sources

As noted by Mitchell (1986), there has been little systematic data collected on the number, type, and prevalence of profit-sharing plans. Therefore, in order to address carefully the question of why firms adopt plans, two new sources of data have been generated: (1) case studies of the determinants of compensation practices in three industries (banking, electronics, transportation equipment), and (2) IRS reports filed by firms with deferred profit-sharing plans in a cross-section of industries. Information about compensation plans in each case-study industry was gathered from existing published sources and a mail survey of firms with more than 200 employees. The response rate to the mailing was between 45 and 50 percent in each of the three industries: a total of 242 responses were received and most contained complete information. Follow-up telephoning of twenty nonrespondents in each industry uncovered no significant differences between respondents and nonrespondents.

The mail survey had several goals: (1) to get an accurate up-to-date census of both cash and deferred profit sharing in each industry; (2) to have firms rate the importance of profit-sharing and pension plans in achieving personnel objectives; and (3) to identify patterns of adoption, termination, and substitution among various deferred payment plans. This third goal was considered important since motives for using plans are often most clearly revealed when changes are made. Table 1 tabulates the plan frequencies from the survey respondents. The figures confirm results from other studies (Metzger, 1964), showing that the majority of larger firms use deferred rather than cash profit sharing. They also illustrate the rapid growth of tax credit ESOPs (PAYSOPs) and 401(k) salary reduction plans,* confirming that tax and regulatory factors have a significant impact on plan choice.

The second new data source consists of six thousand firms in twenty-three two-digit manufacturing, trade, finance, and service industries that filed IRS Form 5500 ("Annual Return/Report of Employee Benefit Plan") for the 1981 tax year. Logistic regressions were run using these data to predict the presence of a profit-sharing and/or pension plan as a function of firm, industry, and regional characteristics. (For a brief discussion of model specification and the main results, see Appendix, page 59.)

Results

Two common reasons given for adopting profit sharing—providing incentives and increasing flexibility—find little support in the evidence gathered. The historical inability of profit sharing to survive recessions is a preliminary indication that plans are adopted for reasons other than to increase flexibility. Balderston (1937) documents the significant increase in plan terminations and reduction in the number of plans established during the Depression. This tendency for profit-sharing plans to be terminated when greater flexibility is apparently required shows up in the case studies. In the banking and electronics industries, there were a substantial number of recent terminations of profit-sharing plans, coinciding with a recession (electronics) and increased levels of competition brought about by deregulation (banking).

Tables 2 and 3 list the terminations, reasons given, year of termination, and the current plans maintained by each firm. Several firms gave reasons for the terminations (for example, indicating that a plan was too "costly" or that contributions had not been made for several years); for other firms, the inference that the terminations were caused by a recession and/or the pressure of increased competition is based on the conversion of profit sharing to 401(k) plans. The 401(k) plan requires employer contributions that are

---

*401(k) plans (named after the section of the tax code which created them in 1978) permit employees to deduct up to 15 percent of current salary (or $30,000, although the monetary limit was reduced in the 1986 Tax Reform Act), placing the money in a tax exempt trust. The employee contribution is frequently matched in whole or in part by the firm. PAYSOPs were created by the 1981 Economic Recovery Tax Act. An employer setting up a PAYSOP was allowed to claim a tax credit for the amount contributed to the PAYSOP trust, up to .5 percent of payroll (.75 percent for 1984–1986). The 1986 Tax Reform Act eliminated the PAYSOP provision.

Percent of Surveyed Firms With Indicated Compensation Plans

Plan	Banking	Electronics	Autos	Aircraft
Number of observations	96	91	29	17
PENSION	94.7%	57.0%	65.5%	88.2%
Defined benefit	89.5	46.1	51.7	82.4
Defined contribution	4.2	6.6	6.9	0.0
Both	1.0	3.3	6.9	5.9
PROFIT SHARING	28.1	47.3	34.5	23.5
Deferred distribution	19.8	27.5	27.6	17.6
Current distribution	3.1	13.2	6.9	0.0
Combined cash and deferred	5.2	6.6	0.0	5.9
EMPLOYEE STOCK OWNERSHIP	39.6	49.5	24.2	41.2
ESOP	7.3	8.8	6.9	0.0
PAYSOP	21.9	20.9	13.8	29.4
Other stock plan	10.4	19.8	3.5	11.8
THRIFT PLAN	76.0	71.4	37.9	76.5
401(k)	59.3	62.6	31.0	41.1
Other thrift plan	4.2	2.2	6.9	11.8
401(k) and other	12.5	6.6	0.0	23.5

COMMON COMPENSATION PLAN CONFIGURATIONS

Plan	Banking	Electronics	Autos	Aircraft
All four plans	4.2	14.3	0.0	11.8
Pension, PS and stock	6.3	0.0	0.0	0.0
Pension, PS and thrift	5.2	4.4	0.0	0.0
Pension, stock and thrift	27.1	13.2	17.2	17.6
Pension and PS	10.4	2.2	6.9	0.0
Pension and stock	1.0	3.3	3.4	0.0
Pension and thrift plan	35.6	13.2	6.9	41.2
Pension plan only	5.2	5.5	31.0	17.6
PS, stock and thrift	0.0	9.9	0.0	5.9
PS and stock	0.0	5.5	0.0	5.9
PS and thrift	1.0	3.3	6.9	0.0
PS only	1.0	7.7	20.7	0.0
Stock and thrift	1.0	2.2	3.4	0.0
Stock plan only	0.0	1.1	0.0	0.0
Thrift plan only	2.1	11.0	3.4	0.0
None of the above	0.0	3.3	0.0	0.0

Table 2:
Status of Terminated Plans in Banking

PROFIT-SHARING PLAN TERMINATED (ALL DEFERRED)

Reason	Converted To	Date	Current Plans
None given	401(k)	1983	MP, PAY, 401(k)
None given	thrift plan	1975	PN, PAY
Not well received by staff	—	1978	PN, PAY, 401(k)
No contribution over the last few years	—	1978	PN, 401(k)
Bank taken over	—	1984	PS (cash), 401(k)
Converted to 401(k)	401(k)	—	PN, Stock, 401(k)
None given	401(k)	1982	PN, 401(k)
None given	pension plan	1958	Thrift, 401(k)
Start pension plan	pension plan	1955	PS (def), 401(k)
Start 401(k) plan	401(k)	1984	MP, 401(k)
Rolled into 401(k)	401(k)	1984	PN, Pay, 401(k)

EMPLOYEE STOCK OWNERSHIP PLAN TERMINATED

Reason	Converted To	Date	Current Plans
Thrift plan established	thrift	1979	PN, 401(k)
None given	—	1982	PN, 401(k)
Start 401(k)	401 (k)	1984	MP, 401(k)
Bank merger	PS plan	—	PN, PS (def), 401(k)
Amended to 401(k)	401(k)	1983	MP, 401(k)

PENSION PLAN TERMINATED

Reason	Converted To	Date	Current Plans
Overfunded	401(k)	1985	401(k)
Converted to thrift	thrift	1984	Thrift, 401(k)
Employer cost and merger	—	1985	PS (def), 401(k)
Merger	—	—	—
Costs outweighed benefits	—	1981	ESOP, 401(k)

KEY:
PN—defined benefit pension plan
MP—money purchase pension plan
PS—profit-sharing plan
SP—stock purchase plan
ESOP—employee stock ownership plan
401(k)—401(k) salary reduction plan
Thrift—thrift plan
PAY—PAYSOP

Table 3:
Status of Terminated Plans in the
Electronics Industry

PROFIT-SHARING PLAN TERMINATED (ALL DEFERRED)

Reason	Converted To	Date	Current Plans
No profits, formula too complicated	—	—	PS (cash), SP, 401(k)
None given	—	1974	PN, SP, Thrift
Set up MP plan, 401(k)	MP, 401(k)	1982	PS, SP, 401(k)
Set up pension	pension	1960	PN, Pay, 401(k)
Drop in employment	—	1984	401(k)
Transferred to 401(k)	401(k)	—	PN, 401(k)
Lack of participation	—	1981	MP, PS (cash), PAY, 401(k)
None given	—	1984	401(k)
Converted to 401(k)	401(k)	1984	401(k)

EMPLOYEE STOCK OWNERSHIP PLAN TERMINATED

Reason	Converted To	Date	Current Plans
Founded 401(k) with stock match	401(k)	—	PN, 401(k)
No profits	—	1985	none
Chapter 11	—	1984	401(k)

PENSION PLAN TERMINATED

Reason	Converted To	Date	Current Plans
Converted to 401(k)	401(k)	1985	401(k)
None given	—	1976	MP, 401(k)
Converted to 401(k)	401(k)	1984	ESOP, 401(k)
Business hardship	—	1982	none
Work force too young	—	1983	ESOP, 401(k)

KEY:
PN—defined benefit pension plan
MP—money purchase pension plan
PS—profit-sharing plan
SP—stock purchase plan
ESOP—employee stock ownership plan
401(k)—401(k) salary reduction plan
Thrift—thrift plan
PAY—PAYSOP

both smaller and linked to matching employee contributions. The regression results also indicate that cyclically stable industries (such as retail trade and transportation as well as service industries in general) are more likely to use profit sharing as the primary source of deferred compensation than cyclically sensitive industries (such as manufacturing).

Cash profit-sharing plans have recently been adopted in several unionized manufacturing industries (for example, autos: Chrysler, Ford, GM; and steel: LTV, Bethlehem) that are in competitive situations similar to those found in banking and electronics. This suggests that flexibility may be a greater factor in the decision to use cash plans, and also that the negative relationship between profit sharing and union activity (see IRS regression results) may be weakening as the generation of union leaders familiar with the abuses of profit sharing in the 1920s retires (Brandes, 1970). Another more cynical interpretation is that profit-sharing plans have little value in these industries, given their depressed state, and were offered by management only as a token benefit in return for substantial wage concessions. The curtailment of the Chrysler plan when the company returned to profitability supports this view; profit sharing may merely have been a temporary stop-gap measure, never regarded by workers as a permanent alternative to wages.

There are several pieces of evidence which indicate that profit sharing is relatively unimportant as an incentive device. First, the pattern of plan substitution shows that profit sharing is frequently replaced by plans with little or no incentive value (for example, fixed payment thrift plans—see Tables 2 and 3). Second, firms themselves rate the incentive value of profit sharing as similar to that of pensions. Table 4 presents average firm ratings of the effectiveness of deferred profit sharing and pension plans in achieving five personnel objectives. The motivational effect of profit sharing is ranked third behind providing retirement income and paying compensation in a tax-wise manner in two of the three industries surveyed. The differences in ratings between pension/thrift and profit-sharing/stock plans are shown in Table 5 for firms with both plans; a negative number indicates profit sharing is more important than pensions in achieving the objective. Profit-sharing/stock plans are viewed as more important than pensions as motivators, but the differences are small and statistically significant only in the electronics industry.

A third piece of (more direct) evidence is the relationship between the occupational distribution in an industry and the prevalence of profit sharing. Since profit sharing is viewed as an

Table 4:
Perceived Effectiveness of Deferred Profit-Sharing Plans By Industry[a]

PERSONNEL OBJECTIVE	BANKING	ELECTRONICS	TRANSPORT. EQUIP.
	Mean	*Mean*	*Mean*
PENSION/THRIFT PLANS			
Recruitment	3.45	3.56	3.31
	(.11)	(.12)	(.18)
Motivation	3.39	3.52	3.29
	(.11)	(.16)	(.19)
Reduction of turnover	2.84	2.94	3.13
	(.11)	(.14)	(.16)
Retirement income	4.70	4.47	4.57
	(.06)	(.09)	(.11)
Tax-wise compensation	3.96	3.88	3.70
	(.11)	(.14)	(.18)
	n = 90	n = 69	n = 44
PROFIT SHARING/STOCK PLANS			
Recruitment	3.37	3.35	3.30
	(.17)	(.16)	(.22)
Motivation	3.55	3.47	3.44
	(.16)	(.17)	(.23)
Reduction of turnover	2.77	2.75	2.90
	(.16)	(.17)	(.21)
Retirement income	3.88	3.47	3.86
	(.17)	(.18)	(.27)
Tax-wise compensation	3.77	3.07	3.65
	(.17)	(.17)	(.25)
	n = 50	n = 57	n = 30

[a]Mean responses to survey question regarding the importance of pension and profit-sharing plans for achieving each listed personnel objective. Scale 1-5 (not important-very important). Standard error of the mean in parentheses.

imperfect, indirect incentive, it should be found where it is difficult to motivate workers using more direct incentive plans (commissions, piece rates, small-group incentives). This includes industries with a heavy concentration of workers whose output is nonstandard and/or involves developing new products (for example, engineers), or those where a larger fraction of workers have some impact on overall profitability (for example, managers). However, the occupational variables in the logistic regressions are generally insignificant. The only statistically significant result is contradictory; profit sharing is actually less likely to be found where managers make up a larger fraction of the work force. One explanation for this result

Table 5:
Comparison of Ratings for Pension vs. Profit-sharing Plans[a]

| | | | TRANSPORT. |
	BANKING	ELECTRONICS	EQUIP.
PERSONNEL OBJECTIVE	Mean	Mean	Mean
Recruitment	−.02	−.11	−.04
	(.22)	(.14)	(.24)
Motivation	−.26	−.40*	−.22
	(.18)	(.14)	(.30)
Reduction of turnover	.04	−.26	.30
	(.17)	(.14)	(.30)
Retirement income	.89*	1.00*	1.00*
	(.19)	(.22)	(.36)
Tax-wise compensation	.02	.56*	.43
	(.20)	(.24)	(.35)
	n = 47	n = 43	n = 23

[a]Differences in mean responses for firms having both pension and profit-sharing plans.
*Significant at 5 percent level.

is that other, more specifically targeted bonus plans are used to motivate managers (such as those based on division or group performance). One bank, for example, noted that it had rejected profit sharing in favor of incentive plans targeted at forty-one separate operating units.

Evidence exists in favor of an alternative explanation for observed patterns of profit-sharing activity: first, that deferred profit sharing is primarily a "pension substitute," that is, another way of making relatively fixed deferred payments; and second, that the observed pattern of profit-sharing and pensions plans is best explained by the influence of past practice in a region and/or industry.

Evidence that profit sharing is primarily a pension substitute is embedded in the case presented against the flexibility motive above. One interpretation of the terminations in electronics and banking is that profit-sharing plans have value only when contributions are positive and stable over time—when they resemble pensions. If this is the case, the only substantial differences between profit-sharing and pension plans is a greater degree of federal regulation of pensions (actual valuations, mandatory contribution levels, pension benefit insurance premiums) and the resulting greater predictability of pensions, since the (nominal) benefit levels are not guaranteed. These regulatory effects can be quite significant; changes in the laws governing thrift plans led to the rapid adoption of 401(k) plans (Table 1), and the passing of ERISA in 1974, which tightened qualifications for all types of deferred payment plans and cut their growth rate in half.

Regulatory factors alone cannot explain patterns of profit sharing across regions and industries, however, since the significant regulations exist at the federal level. The "dispersion hypothesis," or the idea that custom in the local labor market is an important factor, was suggested by a persistent finding that profit sharing is more prevalent in the East. Only in a few instances could firm characteristics other than location (size, profitability, stability of profits, labor intensity) explain plan choice. Table 6 shows this pattern for the electronics industry; in California semiconductor firms, 52 percent have profit-sharing plans as their only deferred payment plan and 14 percent have pensions, compared with 35 percent and 38 percent, respectively, in Massachusetts and Connecticut. This regional pattern is consistent with (1) the gradual spread of pensions from older industries in the East to newer industries in the West, and (2) more frequent adoption of profit sharing where pension plans are less well established. Variables included in the regressions (regional dummies and variables measuring mean plan-establishment dates) provide further confirmation of the dispersion hypothesis. Most of the establishment date variables are statistically significant and of the expected sign. Firms in industries with a longer history of profit sharing are more likely to have profit sharing only; where pensions have been around longer, firms are more likely to have pension plans only. In addition, profit sharing is less prevalent where pensions have been around longer. These effects are significant in absolute terms as well: Moving from an industry where pensions are older on average by five years to one where profit-sharing plans are older raises the prevalence of profit-sharing plans relative to pensions by 25 percent. Finally, the regional dummies reveal a dominance of pensions in the East and profit sharing in the West, similar to the pattern found in the case study industries.

Summary and Policy Implications

Two conclusions emerge from the discussion in the previous section. First, deferred profit sharing is adopted primarily as a pension substitute, with its critical attribute being the provision of a predictable annual contribution. Plans unable to provide stable contributions tend not to survive, and profit sharing is more

Table 6:
Distribution of Compensation Plans by Industry
(California vs. Massachusetts/Connecticut)

| INDUSTRY | BENEFITS | % of firms with indicated plan[a] | |
		CALIF.	MASS./CONN.
SIC code			
3570 Electronic	PS only	80.0	50.0
computing	PN only	20.0	40.0
equipment	Both plans	0.0	10.0
	# of firms	5	10
3665 Radio and TV	PS only	58.3	25.0
receiving equipment	PN only	16.6	50.0
	Both plans	8.3	25.0
	# of firms	12	4
3670 Electronic	PS only	52.4	35.4
components	PN only	14.7	38.7
(semiconductor	Both plans	9.8	9.6
devices)	# of firms	61	31
3815 Scientific	PS only	53.3	32.0
instruments and	PN only	33.3	48.0
measuring devices	Both plans	13.3	20.0
	# of firms	15	25
3698 Misc. electrical and	PS only	57.1	19.4
electronic	PN only	28.5	66.6
equipment	Both plans	4.8	13.9
	# of firms	21	36

[a]Columns may not add to 100% because some firms do not have either type of plan.

KEY:
   PS only: company has only a deferred profit-sharing plan
   PN only: company has only a defined-benefit pension plan
   Both plans: company has both plans

Source: Calculated by author using 1981 returns of IRS Form 5500 (see text).

prevalent in industries with stable profits. Second, the choice of profit sharing over pensions is influenced at least as much by customary practice in the industry or region as by the advantages of profit sharing relative to pensions (for example, flexibility, incentives). These results provide a background for speculation about the future course of profit sharing and the possible impact of policy initiatives on its development.

Cash profit sharing should become more important in the future, even in the absence of policy initiatives. The pattern of diffusion of pension plans indicates that some experience is required before plans begin to spread, and experience with cash profit sharing has begun to accumulate in several highly visible firms and industries. The newly adopted cash plans in several relatively depressed, unionized industries suggest that cash profit sharing is playing more of a role in increasing flexibility than was the case with deferred profit sharing. In addition, resistance to profit sharing from unions (due to the use of profit sharing as a union-busting tool in the 1920s) is diminishing as the generation of union leaders opposed to profit sharing retires.

As for tax policy, firms have demonstrated their sensitivity to tax treatment of income (as witnessed by the rapid growth of 401(k) plans and PAYSOPs in the 1980s); therefore, a significant number of firms can be expected to adopt tax-subsidized plans. The tendency for profit sharing to flourish where profits are stable suggests that if tax advantages are given to cash profit-sharing plans, the first firms and/or industries to adopt them will be those with relatively stable profits. If the firms adopting tax-subsidized profit sharing are those in cyclically stable industries, the macroeconomic benefits of shifting in the direction of a share economy are substantially reduced. Firms adopting profit sharing will already have relatively stable employment, and those with unstable profits and employment will not adopt plans, partly because the resulting fluctuation in compensation would be too great to be acceptable to their workers. This confirms what some skeptics have been saying about Weitzman's share economy proposals (Nuti, 1985); there are no easy and painless ways of increasing wage flexibility enough to stabilize employment.

References

Akerlof, G. "Labor Contracts as Partial Gift Exchange." *Quarterly Journal of Economics* (November 1982): 543–69.

Azariadia, C. "Implicit Contracts and Underemployment Equilibria." *Journal of Political Economy* (December 1975): 1182–1202.

Balderston, C.C. *Profit Sharing for Wage Earners.* New York: Industrial Relations Counselors, 1937.

Belcher, D. *Compensation Administration.* Englewood Cliffs, NJ: Prentice-Hall, 1974.

Brandes, S. *American Welfare Capitalism: 1880–1940.* Chicago: University of Chicago Press, 1976.

Business Trends. *55,000 Largest U.S. Corporations.* Petaluma, CA: Ward Publications, 1981, 1984.

Cheadle, A. "Firm Motives for Adopting Profit Sharing and Employee Stock Ownership Plans." Unpublished Ph.D. dissertation, University of California at Berkeley, 1987.

Conte, M., and A. Tannenbaum. "Employee Ownership: Report to the Economic Development Administration." Washington, DC: U.S. Department of Commerce: Economic Development Administration, 1977.

Czernicki, E. "Effect of Profit Sharing Plans on Union Organizing Efforts." *Personnel Journal* (September 1970): 763–773.

Dempsey, B., and E.J. Lodge. *Revised Profit Sharing Manual.* Akron, OH: Council of Profit Sharing Industries, 1951.

Freeman, R.B. "Effect of Unionism on Fringe Benefits." *Industrial and Labor Relations Review* (July 1981): 489–509.

Knowlton, P.A. *Profit Sharing Patterns.* Evanston, IL: Profit Sharing Research Foundation, 1954.

Kokkelenberg, E., and D. Sockell. "Union Membership in the United States, 1973–1981." *Industrial and Labor Relations Review* 38 (July 1985): 497–543.

Long, R. "The Effects of Formal Employee Participation on Patterns of Organizational Influence." *Human Relations* 34 (1981): 847–876.

Metzger, B.L. *Profit Sharing in Perspective.* Evanston, IL: Profit Sharing Research Foundation, 1964.

Mitchell, D.J.B., and R. Broderick. "Who Has Flexible Wage Plans and Why Aren't There More of Them?" UCLA Institute of Industrial Relations Working Paper No. 119, October 1986.

Nuti, D.M. "The Share Economy: Plausibility and Viability of Weitzman's Mode." Seminar presentation at the Department of Economics, University of California at Berkeley, 1985.

Profit Sharing Council of America. *Profit Sharing Survey.* Chicago: Profit Sharing Council of America, various years.

"Profit Sharing: Now the Difficult Part." *The Economist* (May 17, 1986): 64–66.

Profit Sharing Research Foundation. *Cumulative Growth in Number of Qualified Deferred Profit Sharing Plans and Pensions in the United States: 1939–1982.* Evanston, IL: Profit Sharing Research Foundation (1983).

Rhodes, S., and J. Steers. "Conventional vs. Worker-Owned Companies." *Human Relations* (December 1981): 1013–1036.

Schotta, C. "The Distribution of Profit-Sharing Plans: An Analysis." *Southern Economic Journal* (July 1963): 49–59.

Shapiro, C., and J. Stiglitz. "Equilibrium Unemployment as a Worker Discipline Device." *American Economic Review* (June 1984): 433–444.

Stern, R., and T. Hammer. "Buying Your Job: Factors Affecting the Success of Employee Acquisition Attempts." *Human Relations* (December 1978): 1101–1117.

———. "Employee Ownership: Implications for Organizational Distribution of Power." *Academy of Management Journal* (March 1980): 78–100.

Stern, R.; K.H. Wood; T. Tove; and T. Hammer. *Employee Ownership in Plant Shutdowns: Prospects for Employment Security.* Kalamazoo, MI: Upjohn Institute for Employment Research, 1979.

Tom, P. "High-tech Perks: Benefits in the Silicon Valley." *National Underwriter* (March 30, 1984): 40–41.

Weitzman, M. "Some Macroeconomic Implications of Alternative Compensation Systems." *Economic Journal* (December 1983): 763–783.

———. *The Share Economy: Conquering Stagflation.* Cambridge, MA: Harvard University Press, 1984.

Whyte, W.; T. Hammer; C. Meck; R. Nelson; and R. Stern. *Work Participation and Ownership: Cooperative Strategies for Strengthening Local Economies.* Ithaca, NY: Industrial and Labor Relations Press, Cornell University, 1983.

Appendix

Logistic Regression Procedure

The methodology employed using the IRS data is to model the level of profit-sharing activity as a function of firm, industry, and regional characteristics. *Profit-sharing activity* is defined operationally as the presence of a deferred profit-sharing plan. Other possible indices of profit-sharing activity (percentage of workers covered by plans, percentage of compensation paid via the profit share) were rejected because of concerns about the accuracy of the employee counts reported on the tax forms and the problems of relying on contribution levels from a single year.

The most direct statistical approach to this problem is to fit a logistic (or probit) equation using a random sample of profit-sharing and non–profit-sharing firms. However, all firms are not required to file Form 5500; thus, a representative random sample of non–profit-sharing firms is not readily available. Therefore, the model to be estimated predicts the presence of a profit-sharing plan conditional on the firm having either a profit-sharing or pension plan or both. (Note: Evidence from the case studies confirms that firms view deferred profit-sharing and pension plans as substitutes, but not deferred and cash profit-sharing plans.)

This modified model amounts to the second part of a two-part model, where the first part predicts the presence of some kind of deferred payment plan. The two-part model, frequently used in studies of health care utilization, is an unbiased alternative to Heckman correction techniques for censored data. The second part

Table A-1:
Variable Definitions and Means

VARIABLE	MEAN	STD. DEV.	DEFINITION
Dependent variables			
PSPLAN	.300	.458	= 1 if firm has profit sharing only
PENSION	.543	.498	= 1 if firm has a pension plan only
BOTH	.157	.363	= 1 if firm has both profit sharing and pension
Independent variables			
LARGE FIRM	.187	.390	= 1 if firm has >2500 employees
UNION % (industry)	24.8	19.7	% unionized in two-digit SIC industry, 1980
UNION % (state)	22.7	7.4	% unionized in state, 1980
UNION INTERACTION	5.7	5.2	product of state and industry union variables
UNEMPLOYMENT RATE	7.31	1.65	state unemployment rate, 1980
EMPLOYMENT CHANGE	25.8	18.8	rate of change of state employment, 1970–1980
MEAN PS. EST. DATE (industry)	6.93	2.21	Mean establishment date of profit-sharing plans in sample, by two-digit industry (in years minus 1960, e.g., 7 = 1967).
MEAN PS EST. DATE (state)	6.94	1.96	Mean establishment date of profit-sharing plans in sample, by state.
MEAN PN EST. DATE (industry)	3.14	3.65	Mean establishment date of pension plans in sample, by two-digit industry.
MEAN PN EST. DATE (state)	2.63	1.99	Mean establishment date of pension plans in sample, by state.
% MANAGEMENT	12.93	6.56	% of industry employment in executive, administrative, and managerial positions.
% ENGINEERS	2.41	2.87	% of industry employment in engineering occupations
% TECHNICIANS	2.57	2.01	% of industry employment in technician and related support occupations
% PRECISION PROD	7.73	6.71	% of industry employment in precision production occupations

VARIABLE	MEAN	STD. DEV.	DEFINITION
Industry dummies			
MANUFACTURING	.429	.494	= 1 if firm is in durable manufacturing
TRANSPORTATION	.036	.187	= 1 if firm is in trucking or air transport
COMMUNICATION	.063	.244	= 1 if public utility or radio and TV broadcasting
RETAIL TRADE	.132	.338	= 1 if department store, clothing store, grocery store, or restaurant
FINANCE	.312	.463	= 1 if bank, credit agency, insurance co., or securities dealer
Regional Dummies			
SOUTHWEST	.066	.209	= 1 if Arizona, New Mexico, Texas, or Nevada
CALIFORNIA	.077	.267	= 1 if California
NEW YORK AREA	.195	.396	= 1 if New York, New Jersey, or Pennsylvania
MIDWEST	.201	.401	= 1 if Indiana, Ohio, Missouri, or Illinois
NEW ENGLAND	.095	.293	= 1 if Massachusetts, New Hampshire, Connecticut, Rhode Island, Vermont, or Maine
NORTHWEST	.019	.137	= 1 if Washington or Oregon
GREAT LAKES	.104	.305	= 1 if Michigan, Minnesota, or Wisconsin
MID-ATLANTIC	.045	.209	= 1 if Maryland, Virginia, West Virginia, District of Columbia, or Delaware
SOUTH	.132	.339	= 1 if Georgia, Florida, Alabama, South Carolina, North Carolina, Mississippi, Arkansas, Louisiana, Kentucky, or Tennessee
WEST	.060	.237	= 1 if Montana, Idaho, Utah, Colorado, North Dakota, South Dakota, Iowa, Kansas, Oklahoma, Wyoming, or Nebraska

Sources: **Union variables:** E. Kokkelenberg and D. Sockell, "Union Membership in the United States, 1973–1981, *Industrial and Labor Relations Review*, July 1985, p. 497–543. **Occupation variables:** *Census Supplemental Reports: Detailed Occupation by Industry*, U.S. Bureau of the Census, 1980. **Employment and Unemployment:** *U.S. Statistical Abstract*, 1985. **All other information** (firm size, location, industry): Compilations of IRS Form 5500 by the Department of Labor and calculations by author (see text).

of the model captures most of the important issues, including reasons for adopting flexible or incentive-creating profit sharing versus a fixed-payment pension plan. Further analysis of the first part of the model indicates that factors influencing the choice of profit sharing or pension are relatively independent of the overall decision to adopt a deferred payment plan.

The dependent variable in these regressions is a three-part zero/one variable indicating whether the firm has a pension plan only, profit-sharing plan only, or both profit-sharing and pension plans. Firms with both plans present a problem; theoretically, they should have characteristics "in between" pure profit-sharing and pure pension firms, that is, some need for flexibility/incentives and some need to offer a certain fixed benefit. In practice, firms with both plans are quite different from either pure pension and pure profit-sharing firms; they are larger, with substantially less variation in plan prevalence across regions. In addition, the contribution made to both plans combined is not equal (on average) to the contribution made by firms with one plan, as would be expected if the plans were intended to be complementary.* It is for these reasons that three rather than two categories are used in the logistic models.

The estimates reported in Table A-2 are binomial logistic regressions, predicting the likelihood of the three outcomes conditional on the firm having at least a profit-sharing or pension plan. The relative values of the coefficients across equations are identical to those produced using a multinomial logit procedure. The principal difference in using binomial rather than multinomial techniques (apart from computer cost and program availability) is that the probabilities will not necessarily sum to one. However, simulations based on the estimates in Table A-1 indicate that the predicted probabilities do sum approximately to one.

Two other possible sources of bias in coefficient and standard error estimates, arising because of the choice of modeling procedure, should be noted. First, this choice of logistic regression model assumes the independence of irrelevant alternatives: that taking away one of the choices will not affect the relative selection probabilities of the remaining choices. For example, if the possibility of choosing a pension plan only is taken away, the firm should still have the same relative likelihood of choosing a profit-sharing plan only or both plans together. While it is evident

---

*Regressions relating the level of profit-sharing and pension contribution to the number of plans maintained and other variables showed that the contribution to any one plan is independent of the number of plans maintained; see Cheadle, 1987.

Determinants of Profit Sharing and Pension Plan Participation:
Logistic Regression Coefficients[a]

VARIABLE	PS ONLY	PN ONLY	BOTH
LARGE FIRM	− 27.45**	.35	17.36**
UNION %	− .65*	.37	.12
UNION % (state)	− .16	.26	− .004
UNION INTERACTION[b] (ind x state)	− **	− *	−
UNEMPLOYMENT (% − state)	− 2.89**	3.35	− .94
EMPLOYMENT CHANGE % (state)	.27**	− .17	− .07
% MANAGEMENT (industry)	− 1.23**	.32*	.48
% ENGINEERS (industry)	1.22	− 1.51	.38
% TECHNICIANS (industry)	− 1.55	1.44	.44
% PRECISION PROD (industry)	.42	− .10	− .58
MEANS PS EST. DATE (industry)	− 2.10**	1.88**	− .80
MEANS PS EST. DATE (state)	− 1.99**	2.06**	− .30
MEAN PN EST. DATE (industry)	4.51**	− 2.80**	− .87**
MEAN PN EST. DATE (state)	− 1.13**	.59	.43
INDUSTRY DUMMIES[c]			
PUBLISHING	− .82	− 1.56	− 1.33
TRANSPORTATION	14.04*	− 5.31	− 10.91
COMMUNICATION	.10	− 7.44	− 4.23
RETAIL TRADE	13.71*	− 15.73**	− 5.77
FINANCE	11.29	− 11.71	.47
REGIONAL DUMMIES[d]			
SOUTHWEST	7.32	− 5.58	− 1.49
CALIFORNIA	21.86**	− 21.63**	.35
NEW YORK AREA	− .42	− 1.84	.91
MIDWEST	7.26*	− 7.66*	1.54
NORTHWEST	19.95**	− 18.98**	.71
GREAT LAKES	8.88*	− 11.31**	2.42
MID-ATLANTIC	2.73	− 1.48	− 2.34
SOUTH	8.56	− 5.26	− 1.77
WEST	7.07	− 3.02*	− 3.40
% in category	30.0	54.3	15.7

[a]The figures in the table give the change in probability resulting from a unit change in the independent variable (partial derivative of the logistic function). For example, if the firm is large (greater than 2,500 employees), the probability of its having only a profit-sharing plan is reduced by 27.45 percent.

[b]The asterisks indicate that the union interaction term is significant at the one percent level. The partial with respect to the state and industry union variables is calculated including the interaction term; thus no number is shown for the interaction term itself.

[c]Referenced to manufacturing.

[d]Referenced to New England.

*Significant at the 5% level.

**Significant at the 1% level.

that this assumption may be frequently violated, the direction of the bias for each of the three choices is unclear. The second source of bias arises because observations on individual firms are used as the independent variable while state and industry aggregates are used on the right-hand side. Standard errors estimated for these coefficients will be biased downward if firm errors within the same industry and or region are correlated (as they are likely to be in this case). The magnitude of the bias is uncertain, and of second order importance here, since most of the discussion concerns the relative magnitude of the coefficients.

3. LABOR–MANAGEMENT RELATIONS: UNIONS VIEW PROFIT SHARING

John L. Zalusky

IN MANAGEMENT AND ACADEMIC CIRCLES, profit sharing is seen as an incentive, as a kind of bonding agent between management and labor interests. Lately it has become an element in national employment policy. From organized labor's perspective, profit sharing historically has been an element in employer anti-union behavior. However, it has been and is still viewed as a negotiable benefit, as a means of achieving or maintaining industry wage patterns, and as part of a wage and benefit trade. Recently, labor has begun to view profit sharing as a means of obtaining influence in the corporate decision-making process.

Throughout labor's experience, gaining a voice in the decisions that influence profits and job security has been fundamental to any consideration of profit sharing. Today, that voice is being obtained. To understand organized labor's position on profit sharing, the concept must be viewed in the context of events occurring at the time. To a trade unionist, arguments supporting profit sharing as an incentive, as an economic policy, or for organizational reasons seem weak, unrealistic, or unnecessary. Profit sharing may be seen as less desirable than other options. Thus, instead of providing philosophic support for profit sharing, labor is trying to make practical use of it as a benefit, as a means of maintaining pattern wages, and as a replacement for wages foregone.

This chapter will first discuss profit sharing as viewed by organized labor and then examine labor's reaction to some of the arguments surrounding profit sharing.

Labor's Position on Profit Sharing

As in the case of direct wage incentives and gain sharing, there is no single labor position either for or against profit sharing. Some national unions have opposed the concept; others have supported it and negotiated plans that their members have liked. The majority of unions have dealt with profit sharing on an ad hoc basis without adopting policy statements one way or the other.

However, labor has universally opposed profit sharing when it is used as an alternative to fair wages or as a part of an employer strategy to prevent worker representation. The association of profit sharing with employer abuse has continued throughout the history of profit sharing in the United States. Since the turn of the century, union-represented workers have negotiated profit-sharing plans as an addition to fair wages, in the context of real participation with fair employers. These plans seem to have satisfied both workers and employers. On the other hand, more than one national union has strongly pursued the concept in collective bargaining, only to meet with resistance.

To understand labor's true position on profit sharing, one must look at this issue in its historical context.

Profit Sharing and Labor's Early Experience

Between the 1880s and the 1930s, profit sharing was generally found as part of a brutal package designed to deal with the "labor problem." The other elements usually included "yellow-dog" contracts, "blacklisting," and detective agencies that used spies and *agents provocateurs* who specialized in union busting. The money in profit-sharing accounts was held by the employer, who could refuse individual employees their share. In such a case, the employee had no realistic recourse.

Profit sharing made up a large part of the annual income earned by workers who were covered under these plans, and wages usually fell below those prevailing in the community. The worker expected a large payment at the end of the year. Such payment, however, was in the exclusive control of the employer. If a detective or spy reported that a worker was even seen associating with a trade unionist, the employer could and did implement the provisions of the yellow-dog contract. The worker was not only likely to be fired and blacklisted in the community but also lost a large share of the previous year's earnings contained in the profit-sharing plan.

Considering the brutal industrial relations policies with which profit sharing was associated, it is interesting to note that there were no official policy positions taken against profit sharing by the American Federation of Labor (AF of L) and the Congress of Industrial Organizations (CIO), or later by the AFL-CIO. This was not due to a lack of interest or information. In 1910, a lively discussion of profit sharing appeared in the AF of L's journal, *The American Federationist* (American Federation of Labor, 1910a, 1910b; Shaw, 1910). In 1913, President Gompers noted that employers used profit sharing to prevent their employees' forming a union and to pay them less than a fair wage (Gompers, 1913). In addition, the 1916 strike of 900 workers at the Stetson (hat) Company, which centered on profit sharing versus fair wages, drew a great deal of attention (American Federation of Labor, 1916). There were many other statements by trade unionists against employers who used profit sharing as a means of paying low wages or frustrating worker representation during the period.

Unions and Profit Sharing After the NLRA

The Norris-La Guardia Act of 1932 and the National Labor Relations Act of 1937 outlawed the yellow-dog contracts, blacklisting, and a number of the other noxious practices used by employers. However, profit sharing remained a part of the package used to prevent workers from forming unions.

Nevertheless, labor did not oppose profit sharing. In 1938, AF of L President William Green presented labor's view of profit sharing clearly when he told a Senate committee,

> Labor is not opposed to the principles involved in profit sharing, but is opposed to the way in which it has developed and operated. Profit sharing as developed in the United States was imposed on existing economic injustice and has discouraged union activity to secure a fair basic wage. . . . Labor believes all plans affecting labor must rest on collective bargaining [Green, 1939, 105].

He then described to the committee what he would expect to see in a union-negotiated profit-sharing plan:

(a) Production and Costs records must be equally available to union and management.
(b) Sales policies must be considered by both parties and mutually acceptable. All records must be equally available to both sides.
(c) Salaries of executives and officers and returns to investors must be subject to the same conditions.
(d) Financial policies and proposals must be subjected to the same review and decision.
(e) The standard wages of producing workers, which are production charges, should be fixed by collective bargaining at the highest level industry could be reasonably expected to pay and should provide for customary standards of living proportionate to productivity as human

labor power is increased by mechanical power and machine tools, and reflecting lower unit production costs. The standard wage is the cost item which is the first charge in industry and which is necessary to the sustained consuming power upon which all business depends.

(f) Profit sharing or partnership wage is the share which Labor would have in the net income of the enterprise. In reality, Labor is a partner in production, not from the investment of capital, but from the investment of experience and work ability. As a partner, Labor would have a voice in determining the rates of profit sharing [Green, 1939, 105].

These items are as relevant today as they were nearly fifty years ago.

The only union statement against profit sharing during these hearings was made by John L. Lewis on behalf of the United Mine Workers. At the time, the Mine Workers were assisting the Steelworkers' Organizing Committee, and the steel industry had been trying to use profit sharing to defeat worker representation. For example, one steel firm was described as using profit sharing in connection with its "company union" tactic (Scanlon, 1948). When employees showed interest in organizing an independent union, the employer's tactic was to form a company-dominated union, establish a "profit-sharing" plan, and sign an agreement with the "company union." The workers were then made to understand that if they sought an "outside" union, profit sharing would go with the company union agreement.

Nevertheless, like most unions, the Steelworkers negotiated agreements with profit-sharing plans as early as 1937. However, they were treated as benefit plans that supplemented the basic industry wage and benefit package. United Steelworkers continued to negotiate profit-sharing plans as added benefits (Scanlon, 1948). In 1960, the Steelworkers made 22 agreements with profit-sharing plans (Brubaker, 1960), and in 1985 there were 170 such agreements covering thirty thousand members. (Because of the way the records are kept, these numbers understate the actual prevalence of profit-sharing agreements.) In the 1968 round of basic steel negotiations, profit sharing had become an element of the pattern settlement.

The Textile Workers negotiated profit sharing with the American Velvet Company in 1947 shortly after the War Labor Board limits were lifted. This plan, although modified through negotiations, is still operating. The Amalgamated Clothing Workers of America negotiated deferred profit sharing with Xerox in 1950, dropped it in favor of an assured pension plan, and renegotiated a combined (cash, deferred, and optional stock ownership plan) profit-sharing plan in 1964.*

In a 1949 statement critical of profit sharing, the United Auto Workers (UAW) observed the conditions under which employers offered profit sharing (United Auto Workers-CIO, 1949). Prophetic of the 1979 Chrysler negotiations, the union noted that employers tended to offer profit sharing when there were few or no profits. The UAW paper went on to describe the other basic profit-sharing issues: (1) the plans were not collectively bargained, (2) the union did not have a say (there was no dispute resolution process) in the formula, (3) the union did not have access to the records, and (4) profit sharing threatened the industry-wide wage standards the UAW had struggled to achieve.

Ten years later, on reconsideration, the UAW concluded that profit sharing could be a helpful tool in protecting industry wage and benefit standards through collective bargaining (United Auto Workers, 1958). Profit sharing would systematically distribute gains from the more profitable firms to their workers while maintaining the industry wage and benefit pattern the less profitable firms could afford, as well as the decent standard of living for its members that was embodied in the industry wage and benefit package. Although a sound approach, only American Motors, one of the weaker firms, would agree to profit share in 1961. However, by 1967, the Auto Workers had twenty-one profit-sharing plans, five of which predated the American Motors agreement (Coburn, 1967).

The International Association of Machinists (IAM) has consistently viewed profit sharing suspiciously but without outright opposition. Early in its history, the IAM had negotiated profit-sharing agreements. However, the union became concerned that many employers were trying to use profit sharing as an alternative to sound pension plans and, again, that cash plans were a substitute rather than an addition to basic wages (Newell, 1968). Deferred profit-sharing plans were described as the least desirable of any form of retirement program in the IAM staff letter. Other unions

---

*Profit-sharing plans fall into four categories: (1) cash, with payments made in the current time period, usually shortly after the firm's fiscal year but in some cases quarterly; (2) deferred, with payments made into trust funds to be paid at a later date, generally on retirement; (3) stock purchase, in which shares are used to purchase the firm's stock for the employee's deferred or current account; and (4) combinations in which part of the employee's share is paid out in cash and the rest is used to buy stock or is deferred.

advised caution in negotiations on profit sharing. In an advisory letter to its staff, the International Brotherhood of Electrical Workers cautioned representatives regarding deferred and cash profit-sharing plans and provided guidelines on such negotiations. There have been a number of similar staff advisory letters to national union field staffs on profit sharing over the years.

Descriptive of organized labor's view of profit sharing in the 1940s through the late 1970s are George Meany's remarks in a *Wall Street Journal* article discussing the United Auto Workers proposal for profit sharing in 1958: "There are certain angles to it [profit sharing] that have to be watched very, very carefully. . . . I would not be suspicious of one [profit-sharing plan proposal] that came from the union" (Brone, 1958).

Unions and Profit Sharing in the 1970s and 1980s

There has been a change in labor's approach to profit sharing but no change in the basics. Unions still have to fight employers who are using profit sharing in a strategy that is just as noxious today as it was in the past. In fact, it is so blatant that it has received press coverage. For example, a 1986 *New York Times* article detailed how the owner of Worthington Industries, Inc., a Mr. McConnell, used profit sharing to deprive his employees of their union (Leib, 1986, D-1).

Just as in 1916, workers still want a fair wage before profit sharing and are willing to strike on the issue. This point was driven home in the 1984 Chrysler negotiations. The workers voted to reestablish wage parity with the other auto firms rather than have wages tied to profits. Although there was no strike, the vote was close. The UAW negotiated a new profit-sharing plan, which was implemented in 1988. In the meantime, Chrysler is paying workers a $500 per year lump sum in recognition of Chrysler's profits, the earlier sacrifices made by the workers, and the fact that Ford and GM have profit sharing.

The 1982 Ford and GM agreements include profit-sharing plans, but the UAW had a different experience with Ford and GM from that with Chrysler. Neither firm had Chrysler's problems, yet both had losses or substantial decreases in profits. Both firms negotiated profit-sharing plans when confronted with "take aways." Thus, the profit shares were treated as a replacement for needed wages.

Driven by economic events affecting management, change has occurred with regard to unions and profit sharing, but the pragmatic philosophy of trade unions has not changed. Unions have proposed and used profit sharing to establish or maintain wage and benefit levels, and, as William Green suggested in the late 1930s, to provide meaningful voice in the way the business is operated (Green, 1939). This voice is being obtained by stock ownership, the treatment of wages foregone as debt, joint trusted funds, the right to audits, the right to grieve to arbitration, and union membership on corporate boards.

The 1986 Steelworkers negotiations with LTV established foregone wages as debt that is to be repaid by the use of profit sharing. If profits are insufficient, however, the employer is to issue convertible preferred stock in the parent corporation. Its stock pays dividends of 5 percent. The stock is held in trust for two years, and workers can convert it to voting common stock.

The TWA agreement with the airline pilots and machinists provides employee stock ownership profit sharing. The stock is held in trust by trustees appointed by the union and can be voted. Wage concessions are treated as investments and are paid back from profits.

The UAW agreement with Walker Wire provides the union with the right to audit the books and arbitrate disputes. Arbitration is also provided for in the Steelworker profit-sharing agreement with Blount, a subsidiary of Washington Steel.

A former vice president of the United Auto Workers is on the board of directors of Weirton Steel, an employee-owned enterprise with profit sharing. A union representative is on the board of directors at Wheeling-Pittsburgh Steel, where the restoration of wage concessions is tied to the price of steel and profits.

Thus, if there is a new trend in labor negotiations on profit-sharing plans, it appears to be moving toward gaining influence over management decisions and assuring fair treatment and consideration on a wide range of concerns as well as the condition of the profit-sharing plan.

A Labor View of Other Arguments for Profit Sharing

Trade unionists are interested in improving productivity and working relationships with management, but they also want full participation in the decision process and full employment. However, few see profit sharing by itself as contributing to any of these goals.

Profit Sharing as an Incentive

Like gain-sharing plans, profit-sharing plans are classified as broad-based, indirect incentives; they are even less direct and more broadly based than gain sharing. Gain-sharing benefits are usually paid weekly, monthly, or quarterly. Profit-sharing benefits are usually paid yearly, though a few plans pay quarterly. Thus, profit sharing is more remote in terms of time than are other incentives. Deferred profit sharing, as distinguished from cash profit sharing, is even more remote.

Profit sharing is also a less direct incentive than gain sharing or individual incentives because the factors that affect profits are organizationally separate from the actions of the employees. Also, profits are affected by factors external to the organization and even the nation. Thus profits, profit shares, and rewards to workers may move in directions unrelated to the actions of the plan's participants. An increase in interest rates would push profit shares down, as would a management production decision such as a new Coca-Cola or the Edsel. A change in accounting practices or tax laws can affect the profit shares under many plans; for example, changes in depreciation allowances or inventory pricing will affect profits. Even the way management deals with the press can affect profits as in the incident of glass found in baby food containers. The list goes on, but the fact remains that it is unfair for a worker's earnings to fall because of someone else's actions or mistakes.

If profit sharing comprises a large share of worker earnings, a downturn in profits could have dire results. Workers are likely to vote with their feet by leaving the firm. Recruiting could become more difficult. Wages would have to be increased to retain and obtain workers, offsetting part of profit sharing's advantage to the firm. These events could leave the firm less profitable, worsening an already financially weak condition.

The organizational structure leaves many plan participants outside the decision-making process that affects rewards. Poor management decisions that affect profits and worker shares may produce resentment toward management instead of support—particularly if profit shares are a large part of worker income.

Profit Sharing in Organizational Development

There are a number of underlying ideas supporting and related to the profit-sharing concept in organizational development theory. Most have been relatively unchanged since the eighteenth century.

The basic idea is that workers with a financial tie to the organization will share many of the same goals held by those who own the organization—what is now being called a "common fate" relationship. The idea is often expressed in the use of the term "partnership," with thoughts like "a personal involvement of the individual in the fortunes of the enterprise" and "a common venture with a common gain."

The expectation is that workers with profit sharing will improve productivity, decrease waste, and be more cooperative and thus less committed to an adversarial relationship.

Today, workers are tied to their firms by their jobs. This is a common fate, much more binding to the organization than a small share of the risks and benefits of ownership. In fact, perceived employment security is the major reason many of these plans have been negotiated today, even though the plan is unlikely to provide such security.

Profit Sharing and Management

With few exceptions, management in the 1980s is not interested in either a real or philosophical partnership between capital and labor. Management is concerned with control, and profit sharing can provide some control.

Profit sharing is of interest to modern management because it introduces a form of automatic control over labor costs and, to some extent, because it insulates the decision-makers from the full consequences of their decisions. In a way, profit sharing introduces a form of indexing to labor costs—the linking of some labor costs to internal and external factors, which relieves financial pressure on management by automatically controlling some of these costs. If one considers labor as a factor of production, profit sharing gives management the control and flexibility that it has over few other factors of production. Utility companies do not decrease charges when profits decrease. Because of delinquency and default risks, lenders are more likely to increase interest charges if profits are declining and decrease them if profits are improving—exactly the opposite effect that profit sharing has on labor costs.

Few managements, after receiving this unique accommodation and flexibility from workers, are willing to share with them any real ability to influence the internal decisions and factors that affect profits. For example, in 1986 the former Chief Executive Officer of Eastern Airlines reportedly said that worker representatives have no place on the board of directors. However, in the disruption caused by deregulation and recession, Eastern Airlines employees made severe sacrifices but were able to negotiate employee stock ownership and representation on the board of directors. Thus, it seems that management has no real desire to share control with workers, either as stockholders or as profit sharers unless the organization is on the ropes and has few other options.

Management opposition to worker participation has also taken on a philosophical tone. When the United Automobile Workers demanded profit sharing as a collective bargaining tool in 1958, control became a major issue in business publications. An article in the University of Chicago's *The Journal of Business* concluded: "The diversified character of the issues inherent in the UAW proposal— issues touching parts of the anatomy of the American business- enterprise system—are patent. They are issues ranging from broad philosophies concerning the rights and prerogatives of groups with the social arrangements of production to technical questions of accounting" (Montgomery, Stelzer, and Roth, 1958, 318–334).

Twenty-four years later, essentially the same concerns were raised by Lee Shaw in his address to the Harvard Business School Club of Chicago (1982). However, Shaw raised the additional concern that profit shares "not cut into the money needed for capital investments, research and development, etc." Labor also has these concerns because they affect job security.

Profit Sharing in Macroeconomic Theory

In recent years, the popular press and a few economists have elevated profit-sharing theory to a national economic theory (Weitzman, 1984). A "share economy" is proposed by these advocates as a means of improving productivity and achieving greater wage flexibility, thereby enhancing the nation's competi- tiveness in world markets.

One wishes that those proposing profit sharing in the context of a shared economy had only looked at the history of profit sharing in this country and abroad as well as at the compensation systems in this country that use or have used "work shares."

Many firms have had profit sharing in the past. The record shows no evidence that firms using profit sharing were any more likely to survive recessions or that they created more employment in economic downturns. Many of these firms had dominant positions in their markets, and more than 25 percent of wages were tied to profits. Modern firms that have work shares or have a high percentage of wages tied to profits have encountered serious employee-relations problems when more workers are added in economic upturns. Workers on the rolls do not want to share the added earnings opportunities. Other industrial democracies that have national profit-sharing policies also have employment problems similar to those in the United States.

Enterprises that have work shares have been slow to innovate and adopt new technology. George E. Johnson (1986) reflected on the problem in the context of an economic model of an efficient bargain. The U.S. fishing industry has used work shares for centuries and cannot compete with the factory fishing fleets of the Communist bloc countries, northern Europe, and Japan. Agricultural sharecropping has been all but replaced by corporate forms; jobs have been lost and so have these enterprises.

Consider the pro-cyclical effect of cutting the earnings of workers in half as the economy slides into recession and increasing them by half as the economy expands. To understand the futility of the share economy, we need only look at the abject failure of similar wage-cutting and work-sharing prescriptions for creating jobs during the Great Depression. Wage cuts caused demand to decrease, leading to further profit drops, another round of wage reductions, and on and on in a vicious downward spiral into deeper recession and depression. The prescription of the 1930s destabilized the social structure of the entire country and would have the same consequences today.

Finally, the idea of work shares is unacceptable to working people. They would never support the concept as workers or as voters. The prices workers have to pay for housing, autos, utilities, fuel, and food do not respond in a meaningful way to changes in labor costs. These prices certainly do not change as much or as fast as wages would change, particularly if 50 percent of wages varied with profits, as suggested.

Someone earning $100,000 per year in a nonprofit organization or in government may find profit sharing for private-sector workers to be a good idea, but to the average worker earning $20,000, it is unfair. Cutting the average worker's income to $10,000 because someone else made a poor market decision is unjust. And it would probably cost these workers their homes, autos, higher education for their children, and family unity.

Profit Sharing in Investment Theory

The concept of profit sharing also has implications for investment in a modern industrialized capitalistic society; that is, the competitive model requires profits to investors so as to stimulate investment. If these returns to capital are diverted to labor in significant shares, capital may be more likely to invest elsewhere. Macroeconomic theory, in the long term, would have risk transferred to labor with little or no commensurate return to labor for the risk. Thus, in theory, the return to capital would improve. However, profit sharing is adopted firm by firm, and short-term, almost quarterly, returns on investment are important to stockholders and management. This application does not fit the larger long-term model and is the reason many profit-sharing plans share with workers only after there is a return to equity, and why profit shares to workers comprise a small percentage of total profits.

Lee Shaw (1982) raised the issue of the allocation of returns to capital investment. In the same way that there is no fixed rule on how much of total wages should be related to profit sharing to create worker incentives, there are no guidelines for return on invested capital. The proponents of profit sharing deal with these investment concerns by arguing that profit sharing is a dynamic concept—that is, that the improved relationship between employees and the organization will result in enough increased profits to more than offset the lost return to investors. However, there is no general evidence that profit sharing has improved labor productivity enough to offset the share of profits going to work force.

Shaw's concern is more rhetoric than substance; management does a good job of looking out for its own interests and those of the stockholders. Most profit-sharing plans set aside a fixed percentage for return to capital before building a profit-sharing fund, and then share a percentage of additional profits. Thus, the proportion of corporate earnings going to profit sharing is generally a very small portion of total profits and is paid after a sound return on capital is satisfied. For example, Ford's profit sharing was 9 percent of total profits before taxes and GM's was 5 percent in 1984, a reasonably good year for both firms.

The Profit-sharing Dilemma

How large should profit shares be to retain a flow of investment capital and still provide worker incentive without adverse side effects? This question produces a dilemma. If profit shares are small, they may provide no real incentive. Yet, if they are large, they could become a disincentive and have an adverse effect on investment. In 1980, the Profit Sharing Research Foundation concluded that profit-sharing plans should contribute 8 percent of earnings to balance the various interests and still provide incentives to workers and investors.

A study of profit-sharing plans by Hewitt Associates in 1979 (a high corporate profit year) found that the average profit share was nearly 10 percent of wages. At the upper end, a few firms had 45 percent of wages tied to profits. One union negotiated plan had profit shares and gain sharing making up 60 percent of annual earnings. Average earnings in this firm of highly skilled workers were $30,000 in 1985.

Future for Profit Sharing

Labor has never been convinced that carrot-and-stick incentives are necessary or desirable for American workers or that there is a problem with the bond between management and labor. However, to the extent that management adopts these incentives, profit sharing seems an ineffective incentive and bonding agent compared with other types of programs. Gain sharing and stock ownership seem more effective on all counts.

In micro- and macroeconomic theory, profit sharing presents practical problems for the firm and for the nation. The firm problems are manageable on a case-by-case basis, but the large-scale adoption of work sharing or the share economy offers workers only shared hardship.

However, trade unions have considered and will continue to consider profit sharing in solving particular collective bargaining problems, but profit sharing is not a goal in itself.

Today, labor is not only a partner through its labor and skills; it is investing wages and benefits, too, while in some cases, it is treated as investment and in others as debt. The result is the same: Labor will "have a voice."

When labor-management relationships have stabilized in the future, the past few years will be identified by the trade unions as movement outside the bounds of the traditional collective bargaining framework. Look at labor's changing role in the corporate decision-making process over the last five years. Consider the UAW understanding with GM on the Saturn Plant, the TWA agreements, and the National and LTV steel agreements. Years from now, profit sharing may well be seen as the more traditional part of the whole partnership package.

References

American Federation of Labor. "Another View of Mr. Shaw's Proposition." *American Federationist* 17 (1910): 517.

Brone, R. "Meany Says Reuther's Profit-sharing Proposal 'Will Have to be Watched.' " *The Wall Street Journal* 9 (February 4, 1958): 9.

Brubaker, O. Letter to K.M. Thompson (January 26, 1960).

Coburn, C.L. Letter to E.R. Carnecki (November 30, 1967).

Gompers, S. Letter to J.G. Palmer (February 17, 1913).

Green, W. "Survey of Experiences in Profit Sharing and Possibility of Incentive Taxation." *Hearings Before a Subcommittee of the Committee on Finance.* Washington, DC: Government Printing Office, 1939, 105–107.

Johnson, G.E. "Work Risks, Featherbedding, and Pareto-optimal Union-management Bargaining." Cambridge, MA: National Bureau of Economic Research, Inc., Working Paper No. 1820, 1986.

Leib, J.A. "The Promise of Profit Sharing, " *The New York Times* (February 9, 1986): 10.

Montgomery, R.E.; R. Roth; and I.M. Stelzer. "Collective Bargaining over Profit Sharing: The Automobile Union's Efforts To Extend Its Frontier of Control." *Journal of Business of the University of Chicago* 31 (1958): 318–334.

"Mr. Shaw's Scheme of Capitalizing Labor." *American Federationist* 17 (1910): 687.

Scanlon, J.N. "Profit Sharing Under Collective Bargaining: Three Case Studies." *Industrial and Labor Relations Review* 2 (1948): 58–75.

Shaw, L. "Remarks on Union-negotiated Profit-sharing Plans," (at Harvard Business School Club of Chicago). *Daily Labor Report* (March 24, 1982): E1–E6.

Shaw, W. "Can Labor Be Capitalized?" *American Federationist* 17 (1910): 524.

"Stetson Strike and Profit Sharing." *American Federationist* 23 (1916): 383.

United Auto Workers Administrative Letter 10 (1958): 3.

United Auto Workers-Congress of Industrial Organization, Research and Engineering Department. "What's Wrong with Profit-sharing Plans." *UAW-CIO Facts for Action* 1 (1949): 1–2.

Weitzman, M.L. *The Share Economy: Conquering Stagflation.* Cambridge, MA: Harvard University Press, 1984.

4. EMPLOYEE STOCK OWNERSHIP PLANS: CONSEQUENCES FOR PARTICIPATION AND PERFORMANCE*

Raymond Russell, Patrick G. Grasso, and Terry J. Hanford

IN 1974, THE U.S. GOVERNMENT embarked on an ambitious program to encourage the formation of employee stock ownership plans (ESOPs) in American firms. Since the inception of this program, some observers have seen in ESOPs the potential to bring about unprecedented increases in employees' participation in both the financial rewards and the governance of their firms. By accumulating shares of sponsoring company stock in the retirement accounts of employees, ESOPs give each employee a lasting and growing stake in the profits of a firm. As the portion of each company's stock that is owned by the ESOPs increases over time, ESOPs could give employees a substantial, perhaps even controlling, ownership interest in the firms that employ them. This could have major implications for corporate governance. In addition, supporters have argued that ESOPs could promote improvements in corporate productivity and profitability because of the financial stake they give employees in the success of sponsoring firms.

To what extent have ESOPs actually provided financial rewards to employees, encouraged increased employee participation in management, and improved corporate economic performance? The U.S. General Accounting Office (GAO) has recently completed a major study of ESOPs that has provided answers to many important questions about these plans. In this paper, we will focus particularly on GAO's findings on the extent to which ESOPs have increased employees' participation in the ownership and governance of their firms and on the effect of ESOP sponsorship on the financial performance of those firms. First, however, we provide information about the origins and the growth of these plans.

---

*The views and opinions expressed by the authors are their own and should not be construed to be the policy or position of the U.S. General Accounting Office.

Origins of ESOPs

In his book *The Share Economy,* published in 1984, Martin Weitzman described a novel system of profit sharing that had the potential to combat both inflation and economic stagnation at the same time. While Weitzman's proposal attracted a good deal of attention in both academic circles and the popular press, most commentators were apparently unaware that San Francisco attorney Louis Kelso had been making similar claims on behalf of employee stock ownership for nearly thirty years (Kelso and Adler, 1958, 1961; Kelso and Hetter, 1967; Kelso and Kelso, 1986). Unlike Weitzman's ideas, Kelso's proposals have been incorporated into national economic policy since 1974 and have already been adopted by thousands of American corporations that together account for many millions of employees.

In a work entitled *The Capitalist Manifesto* (1958), Kelso and Mortimer Adler argued that what America most needed was for its workers to earn more income in the form of profit and less in the form of wages. If workers had a greater financial stake in corporate profits, the authors reasoned, they would become less insistent on seeking wage increases, which are inflationary, and more eager to increase the profits upon which the health of the economy depends. To help bring this about, the authors recommended a wide range of measures, including the encouragement of equity-sharing plans in corporations that make stockholders of employees, the adoption of legislation requiring mature corporations to pay out all of their earnings in the form of dividends to stockholders, and the abolition of the corporate income tax.

In 1967, Kelso and Patricia Hetter introduced a new technique for promoting employee stock ownership. The work was entitled *How To Turn Eighty Million Workers into Capitalists on Borrowed Money.* Relying solely on existing tax law, the book offered corporations a way both to promote employee stock ownership and to save money on taxes at the same time. The key to these tax savings was for a corporation in need of capital to have its employee benefit plan take out a loan and then use the loan proceeds to purchase an equivalent amount of company stock. The stock thus purchased would serve as collateral for the loan, and the company would then make annual contributions to the plan sufficient to cover the payments on the loan. The tax advantage that would result consisted in the fact that the corporation could deduct the principal as well as interest from its taxable income as it repaid the loan.

These ideas languished in relative obscurity until Kelso was introduced to Senator Russell Long in 1973. Long was then serving as chair of the powerful Senate Committee on Finance, which was in the process of drafting the Employee Retirement Income Security Act of 1974 (ERISA). The initial draft of this legislation would have discouraged employee benefit plans from investing their assets in their own company's stock, and would have prohibited the kinds of "leveraged" transactions that Kelso had advocated in 1967. Thanks to the Kelso–Long connection, however, the bill's final version explicitly encouraged the formation of employee stock ownership plans and made them the only employee benefit plans that legally could use their assets as security for loans. In the years after 1974, Long was instrumental in convincing Congress to pass legislation that added a number of other important incentives for corporations to form ESOPs, including a variety of tax deductions and tax credits (see Rosen, Klein, and Young, 1986, pp. 251–253; U.S. General Accounting Office, 1986b, pp. 57–9).

The GAO Study of ESOPs

By 1984, the federal ESOP program was ten years old, but both the general public and the federal government remained largely ignorant about what had been the impact of that program on American corporations. It was at this point that Senator Russell Long requested the U.S. General Accounting Office to conduct a thorough study of these plans. That study has provided answers to many important questions about ESOPs.

The data used in this study came from three sources: the Employee Plan Master File (EPMF) maintained by the IRS on all employee benefit plans, a two-wave mail survey of firms that sponsor ESOPs, and corporate tax returns for a selected subsample of ESOP sponsoring firms and a matched sample of non-ESOP companies. IRS provided GAO with EPMF data for the period 1974 to 1984 on all plans for all firms that identified at least one of their employee benefit plans as having "ESOP features." In January 1985, GAO surveyed a nationally representative stratified random sample of 2,004 plans tentatively identified as ESOPs. A total of 1,616 plans (81%) responded to this survey, of which 1,113 turned out to be active ESOPs. A second, more detailed questionnaire was administered to the corporate sponsors of these plans, of which 860 (77%) responded.

On the basis of this survey, the GAO estimated that approximately 4,100 ESOPs were active in 1983, with a total of more than seven million participating employees (U.S. General Accounting Office, 1986a, pp. 8–9, 22–23). (This figure for the total number of ESOPs is lower than some previous estimates, but it excludes more than seven hundred ESOPs that had been terminated, and also omits an even greater number of stock bonus plans that are like ESOPs in many respects.) In addition, an estimated 625 ESOPs were formed between 1984 and March of 1986, for a total of nearly five thousand ESOPs as of the latter date (U.S. General Accounting Office, 1986b, p. 18).

Of greater relevance for present purposes, the GAO has also collected a great deal of data on the various ways in which ESOPs might have affected the behavior of their firms. These include data on the forms and extent of employee participation that occur within ESOP firms, and on the effects of ESOPs on the economic performance of their firms.

Employee Financial Participation in ESOP Firms

In the eyes of Louis Kelso, the main thing wrong with the American economy today is that Americans earn too much of their incomes in the form of wages, and derive too small a portion of their income from the profits upon which the health of our economy depends. As a result, working Americans are too eager to increase wages and have too little regard for the profitability of their firms. To alleviate this perceived problem, Kelso has long advocated employee ownership and similar arrangements as a means of providing every American with a "second income" that would come in the form of profit instead of a wage.

The GAO study gives little indication that ESOPs have provided the basis for such a profit-based income to date. GAO found that the median value per participant in ESOP trusts was only about $5,200 in 1983 (U.S. General Accounting Office, 1986a, p. 23). This amount appears to fall short of what is required to provide a meaningful source of income, as proposed by Kelso. One problem is that in most corporations the income generated by that quantity of stock is unlikely to amount to more than a few hundred dollars per year, and therefore in all probability continues to pale in significance when compared to a worker's wage.

A second major problem is that in most cases the income generated by this ESOP stock is not distributed to employees, but instead either is reinvested in the corporation in the form of retained earnings, or if paid out as dividends is added to employees' ESOP accounts. The GAO found that 58 percent of all corporations with ESOPs never pay dividends. Of those corporations that had paid dividends prior to June of 1984, only 8 percent distributed dividends on ESOP stock directly to employees. In the other 92 percent of dividend-paying firms, the dividends associated with ESOP stock were simply added to the balances in employees' ESOP accounts (U.S. General Accounting Office, 1986b, p. 37). As a result the hypothesized second income generated by their stock in the ESOPs remains for most employees a remote promise for the future rather than a meaningful supplement to current cash earnings.

In order to encourage corporations with ESOPs to pay more dividends directly to employees, the Deficit Reduction Act of 1984 (DEFRA) included a provision allowing corporations to deduct from their incomes all dividends paid out to participants on stock held in ESOPs. However, among ESOPs that had held dividends in plan trusts prior to this legislation, only 5 percent indicated to GAO in 1985 that they had begun to pay out dividends after its passage.

Although ESOPs have so far fallen short of creating the kind of immediate link between corporate profits and employees' incomes that Kelso initially had in mind, it would probably be a mistake to conclude that the stock being accumulated in employees' ESOP accounts is without significance for their relationship to their firms. For example, the financial stakes created by the ESOPs give employees the potential to earn substantial long-term capital gains over the period of their employment, even if they do not yield much income in any given year. An ESOP may also make employees more interested in a firm's current profits, because the size of the firm's annual contributions to the ESOP is often a function of the profitability of the firm. It also is possible that the ESOPs have an important symbolic value, helping to give employees a feeling that they and managers are on the same side, even if each employee's personal stake in the company's current profits is not very large.

The results of a recent survey of employees in 37 companies with ESOPs are illustrative in this regard. The sample of companies was selected by the National Center for Employee Ownership (NCEO). It deliberately included companies in which the ESOP owns an unusually high proportion of the company's stock: on average, the 37 companies in the survey owned 42 percent of the equity in their firms. Aided by this conducive circumstance, 84 percent of employees in these companies agreed with the statement, "Owning stock in this company makes me more interested in the company's financial success." A smaller but still substantial 65 percent of employees in these companies also agreed that "Employee ownership at this company gives me a greater share in company profits" (Rosen, Klein, and Young, 1986, p. 90). In the majority of ESOPs, where employees' equity stakes are generally smaller, the percentage of employees agreeing with such sentiments would probably be lower than this, but is unlikely to be negligible.

Employee Participation in Decision Making in ESOP Firms

In general, legislation does not require that firms sponsoring ESOPs provide their employees with opportunities to participate in corporate governance. Nevertheless, many students of ESOPs have suggested that these plans offer the possibility of extensive employee control over or participation in the management of sponsoring companies. Some further argue such participation as a way to encourage employee efforts to improve productivity and profitability. On the other hand, some have expressed concern that ESOPs could result in excessive employee control over corporate management, to the detriment of the firm's financial health. Such concerns have been cited as a major impediment to the more rapid spread of ESOPs.

The responses to GAO's survey suggest that the impact of ESOPs on decision making in sponsoring firms has so far fallen well short of the revolutionary implications that have sometimes been ascribed to them. First, ESOPs generally own only a small percentage of the voting shares in the sponsoring companies. In 1985, the median ESOP owned just 5 percent of its firm's voting stock, and only 19 percent of ESOPs owned 25 percent or more of their firm's voting stock.

Second, most ESOPs do not pass through the voting rights connected with their stock to individual employees, but instead allow those rights to be exercised by plan trustees. Federal law requires a full pass through of voting rights only in publicly traded firms. The GAO found, however, that most ESOPs (76 percent) are sponsored by privately traded firms (U.S. General Accounting Office, 1986a, p. 19), which are required to pass through voting rights only in certain circumstances.

Third, ESOP arrangements usually do not include employee representation on the corporation's board of directors. Representatives of unions or nonmanagerial employees were elected to serve on the boards of directors of only 4 percent of ESOP firms in the GAO study, and in no case did a firm report that such representatives held a majority of the seats on its board.

Other evidence suggests that ESOPs exert only a modest impact on company boards even when the ESOPs own a majority of their firms' voting stock and pass through full voting rights to their employees. The NCEO reported that in a study of sixteen such firms, rank-and-file employees were entirely absent from the boards of six, and constituted only a minority on the other ten boards. In only two of the sixteen companies did it appear that the presence of nonmanagerial employees on the board of directors had had a substantial impact on decision making in a sponsoring firm (Ivancic and Rosen, 1986).

Fourth, the GAO data also shed light on the extent to which the ESOPs have increased employee participation in decision making in other ways. For example, one question in the survey asked respondents to compare the current involvement of nonmanagerial employees to its level before the ESOP was introduced. Only 27 percent of ESOPs reported that the involvement of nonmanagerial employees was greater now than it had been before the ESOP was established; 68 percent said that employee involvement had remained unchanged; and one percent indicated that employee involvement had actually declined (another 4 percent of ESOPs did not respond to this item).

The 27 percent of ESOPs that indicated that the involvement of nonmanagerial employees had increased after the ESOP was introduced were asked whether this increase had occurred "mostly through informal means such as casual meetings or conversations," or "mostly through formal means such as new committees or task forces." Of the ESOPs that answered this question, 76 percent reported that the increase in employee involvement had occurred through informal means. Only 23 percent of those respondents, or 6 percent of all ESOPs, indicated that an increase in employee involvement had occurred through formal means, or through a combination of formal and informal means. It thus appears that the ESOPs have produced largely increases in informal employee involvement in decision making, and have done that only in about a quarter of all ESOP firms.

Finally, respondents were asked to identify the specific issues, if any, that are addressed by work groups or committees involving nonmanagerial employees in their firms. (See Table 1.) The issues most frequently mentioned were generally shop floor issues such as safety; working conditions, job design, and quality of working life; maintaining good relations between management and employees;

Table 1:
Issues Addressed by Nonmanagerial Employees
Within ESOP Firms

Safety	42%
Working Conditions, Job Design, and Quality of Working Life	34%
Maintaining Good Relations Between Management and Employees	33%
Reducing Production Costs	30%
Quality Circles	19%
Developing New Products or Services	14%
Strategic or Long Range Planning	13%
Budgeting and Financial Control	11%

Source: United States General Accounting Office, 1986b, p. 42.

and reducing production costs. Only rarely, however, did nonmanagerial employees become involved in higher-level decisions, such as developing new products or services, strategic or long range planning, or budgeting and financial control.

For the 55 percent of ESOPs that indicated nonmanagerial employees participate in decisions in one or more of the issue areas discussed above, GAO asked an additional question designed to pin down more specifically the nature of nonmanagerial employees' involvement in those issues. Did nonmanagerial employees "receive information only," "offer suggestions and opinions," "make decisions with management," or "make decisions on their own"? Companies were encouraged to check all of these categories that applied in their firm. Nearly all firms responding (95 percent) indicated that they elicit suggestions from employees, but in only 10 percent do employees make decisions on any of these matters on their own, and in only 33 percent do they share decision making with management.

Thus, by almost any measure, ESOPs have played only a quite modest role in increasing the levels of nonmanagerial employee involvement in decision making that occurs within their sponsoring firms.

Effects of ESOPs on the Economic Performance of Sponsoring Firms

Many ESOP proponents have argued that firms could experience notable improvements in economic performance through ESOP sponsorship. The rationale often put forward is that ESOPs give workers an ownership stake in the success of their firms that can act as a powerful motivator for employees to initiate or support actions that lead to higher productivity growth and profits. On the other hand, some analysts have argued that ESOPs are unlikely to provide strong motivation because they constitute a weak form of ownership. Not only is the workers' stock held in a retirement trust, but dividends are seldom paid directly to participants, voting rights often are restricted, and participation in corporate decision making is limited.

A number of studies have tried to measure the effects of ESOP sponsorship on corporate performance. The results have been mixed and inconclusive. Some studies have concluded that ESOPs may improve corporate performance (Conte and Tannenbaum, 1978; Marsh and McAllister, 1981; Rosen and Klein, 1983; Wagner and Rosen, 1985; Trachman, 1985; Cohen and Quarrey, 1986; Quarrey, 1986). Others, however, have found no difference between the performance of ESOP companies and that of similar non-ESOP firms (Tannenbaum, Cook and Lohmann, 1984; Bloom, 1985).

A major limitation of most of these studies is that they lack an adequate basis of comparison for forming their conclusions. While some compare the performance of ESOP and non-ESOP firms, most do not include data on each group both before and after ESOP formation. Besides the GAO study only two other studies of the economic effects of ESOPs have taken this step. The first (Bloom, 1985) found that ESOPs had no effect on either productivity (measured as sales per employee and employment growth) or profitability (gross return on capital). But that study dealt almost exclusively with publicly traded companies, whereas most ESOP firms are small and privately held. The second (Quarrey, 1986) did find higher rates of growth in sales and employment for ESOP firms, but that study was based on a small, non-representative sample and did not directly address issues of productivity and profitability.

The GAO study addressed the issue of ESOP effects on corporate performance using a quasi-experimental design and financial data derived from corporate tax records. A subsample of ESOP firms which began sponsoring their plans during the period 1976–79 was selected for analysis. This time period was selected to insure that GAO could collect financial information for a six-year period (from two years before the ESOP's initiation to three years after) for each firm. For each ESOP firm, a comparison firm without an ESOP was selected using information maintained by the Statistics of Income Division of IRS. The pairs of firms were matched by principal business activity code, and by size (measured as total receipts). Financial data for each firm were taken from corporate income tax returns. (Since most of the firms were privately held, annual stockholder reports generally were not available.)

The initial sample consisted of 414 ESOP and matched non-ESOP firms, but several factors relating to the heavy burden of data collection greatly reduced the usable sample. First, IRS could provide the required six consecutive tax returns for only 111 pairs of firms, either because one of the firms did not file returns for all the years covered or because the returns were unavailable for administrative reasons. Second, many of the returns were missing needed data. These problems left a usable sample of 102 pairs of firms for the profitability analysis, and 44 for the productivity analysis reported below.

The major analyses looked at the effects of the ESOP on the productivity and profitability of the sponsoring firm, with the performance of the non-ESOP firm acting as a control. Physical measures of productivity often are difficult to derive, but a commonly used ratio is value added to product divided by some index of labor input. For this study, value added was divided by total labor compensation (salaries and wages plus benefits), where both the numerator and denominator had been adjusted using industry-specific deflators. The resulting ratio, real value added per unit labor cost, approximates a physical productivity measure.

Tax return data provided all the information needed to construct a measure of profitability. In this case, GAO used the ratio of after-tax income to fixed assets (return on assets). Because interest payments on business loans are deductible from pre-tax income but dividend payments on corporate stock are not, two firms with identical pre-tax income could have different after-tax income if one raised its capital primarily by borrowing and the other by issuing stock. To remove this potential source of bias, GAO deducted the value of the "tax shield" for borrowed funds (interest payments multiplied by the marginal tax rate) from after-tax income before dividing by the value of assets.

The major finding of the GAO study was that ESOPs did not appear to improve the productivity or profitability of sponsoring firms. A glance at Figures 1 and 2 makes clear that the ESOP firms in the subsample performed at about the same level as the non-ESOP firms. Statistical analyses of the data using analysis of covariance (ANCOVA) and multivariate analysis of variance (MANOVA) generally found no statistically significant differences between ESOP and non-ESOP firms. (The only statistically significant finding was that ESOPs formed in 1976–77 outperformed matched non-ESOP firms on profitability during the second year after ESOP formation; but this difference disappeared in the third year, and may have been a statistical artifact.)

Finally, GAO looked at some of the factors that might affect whether ESOP sponsorship could have an impact on performance in given firms. From a variety of data sources, GAO developed

Figure 1:
Median Profitability Before and After
Sponsoring an ESOP[a]

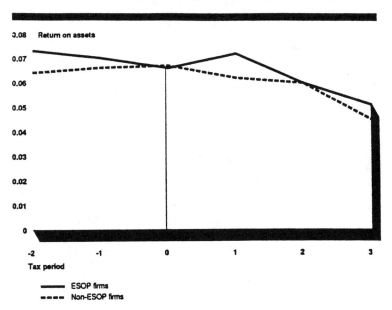

[a]The central vertical at 0 represents the tax period when an ESOP was adopted. N = 102 pairs of ESOP and non-ESOP firms.

Source: U.S. General Accounting Office, 1987, p. 16.

Figure 2:
Median Productivity Before and After
Sponsoring an ESOP[a]

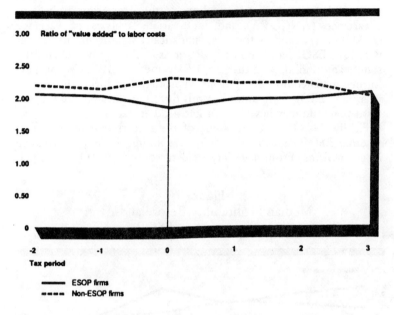

[a]The central vertical at 0 represents the tax period when an ESOP was adopted.
N = 44 pairs of ESOP and non-ESOP firms.

Source: U.S. General Accounting Office, 1987, p. 23.

indicators of the structure of the ESOP (whether it was established under the terms of ERISA or under subsequent legislation providing tax credits for certain ESOPs), the extent of ownership (assets per participant in the ESOP trust), employee ownership and influence exercised through the ESOP (percent of the firm's stock held by the ESOP, whether participants have full voting rights, the *level* of employee participation in corporate management, and the *change* in such participation after the ESOP was established), and corporate context (industry and size of firm). Each of these factors has been hypothesized to affect the extent to which ESOPs might improve corporate economic performance.

GAO estimated regression models relating changes in productivity and profitability (pre-ESOP versus post-ESOP) to the variables discussed above. The results, shown in Table 2, indicate that most of these variables were not related to changes in corporate performance. (The sample sizes underlying this table differ from those for Figures 1 and 2 primarily because of the attrition of firms that did not provide necessary data through the GAO survey. On the other hand, in a few cases ESOP firms excluded from the earlier analyses because of missing data on the matching firms are added back for this analysis.)

The one exception is of special interest for our purposes because it indicates that the higher the *level* of employee participation in corporate management, the greater the improvement in corporate productivity. (Note that the same result does not apply to any *change* in the level of participation after an ESOP was introduced, however.) This finding is associational, not causal; it is not clear whether ESOP firms that give their employees greater voice in decision making show more improvement, or whether ESOP firms that are performing well give their employees more opportunities to participate. Moreover, even if participation is a key variable in improving productivity, ESOP sponsors are not required to provide for such participation, and in any event a firm can have a participative management program without sponsoring an ESOP.

Table 2:
Factors Related to Changes in ESOP Firm Performance

Independent variables	Profitability		Productivity	
	Coefficient	S.E.	Coefficient	S.E.
(Constant)	.57	1.10	−.40	.25
Type of ESOP	.94	.97	.20	.21
Assets per participant	.00	.00	−.00	.00
Percent owned by ESOP	−.02	.03	−.00	.01
Full voting rights	−.24	.91	.21	.20
Level of participation	−.87	.97	.52[a]	.21
Change in participation	−1.22	.83	.25	.18
Industry	.58	.74	.24	.17
Size (revenues)	−.00	.00	−.00	.00
R^2	.07	3.10	.23	.49
Number of cases	80		47	

[a]Significant at the .02 level.

Source: United States General Accounting Office, 1987, p. 31.

Why Do Firms Sponsor ESOPs?

If most ESOPs do little to increase employees' participation in decision making or in profits, or to improve the economic performance of their firms, then why do firms sponsor them? A number of alternative uses of ESOPs have frequently been featured in articles that have appeared in the nation's business press. Many stories, for example, have called attention to the use of ESOPs to prevent the closure of a plant, or to make a firm less vulnerable to hostile takeover attempts.

GAO found, however, that while they may make interesting stories, these purposes also have had far less to do with the spread of the ESOPs than a number of less newsworthy ends. When asked to select the "major reasons" that had led to the decision to form an ESOP in their firms, few respondents indicated that they had formed their ESOP to save the company from going out of business, or to bolster their firm against a hostile takeover attempt (see Table 3). Similarly, few respondents reported forming an ESOP in order to discourage unionization or in exchange for wage concessions from employees.

Turning to the responses that figured more prominently in the answers that GAO received, the most popular choice by far was to indicate that the ESOP had been formed to "provide a benefit for

---

Table 3:
Why Firms Form ESOPs

To Provide a Benefit for Employees	91%
For the Tax Advantages	74%
Improve Productivity	70%
Buy Stock of a Major Owner	38%
Reduce Turnover	36%
Transfer Majority Ownership to Employees	32%
Raise Capital for Investment	24%
Decrease Absenteeism	14%
Avoid Unionization	8%
Make Firm Less Vulnerable to Hostile Takeovers	5%
Save Failing Company	4%
Exchange for Wage Concessions	3%
Take Company Private	1%

Source: United States General Accounting Office, 1986b, p. 20.

employees." This response may simply reflect the legal requirement that all employee retirement plans must be formed for the exclusive benefit of employees. But the prominence of this avowed purpose for sponsoring an ESOP also may help to explain why ESOPs have not done more to increase employees' participation in the financial performance or the governance of their firms. For if employers view their ESOPs predominantly as retirement plans, then it becomes easy to understand why employers prefer to allow the dividends in employees' ESOP stock to accumulate in their retirement accounts instead of being paid out to the employees. And insofar as employees' stockholdings are viewed as retirement assets to be protected rather than as vehicles to increase employees' involvement in the governance of their firms, it is also consistent to leave the voting of ESOP shares in the hands of plan trustees.

After providing a benefit for employees, the second most commonly cited purpose was to utilize the tax advantages associated with ESOPs. The popularity of this alternative clearly supports the common impression that ESOPs are a tax-driven reform. Interestingly, however, GAO found that less than half of all ESOPs that had been formed by the end of 1983 had actually made use of either of the two best-known tax incentives for forming ESOPs that had been established prior to 1984. These are the ESOP leveraging provision, which had been made available in 1974, and the ESOP tax credit, which began in 1975 and was available for certain ESOPs. (The tax credit was repealed in 1986.)

Of the ESOPs in existence at the end of 1983, the GAO found that only 16 percent had ever used the leveraging provision, while another 26 percent had claimed the ESOP tax credit. The remaining 58 percent of ESOPs had never taken advantage of either of these two tax incentives. (However, they all utilized the provisions allowing a deduction from corporate income for contributions to an employee plan and the deferral of personal income taxes on plan trust earnings.) However, 35 percent of ESOPs had written the capacity for leveraging into the design of their plans (U.S. General Accounting Office, 1986a, p. 9), suggesting the possibility of broader use of this provision in the future.

The third most popular choice was to report that an ESOP had been formed in order to improve productivity in a firm. Many firms that had hoped to gain productivity improvements from their ESOPs may have been disappointed, however, because as we have already noted, ESOPs do not appear to lead to higher rates of productivity growth.

Perhaps the most interesting finding of this portion of the GAO study involves the purposes that appeared in fourth and sixth place.

Thirty eight percent of respondents reported that they had established their ESOP to buy the stock of an existing major stockholder or owner, and 32 percent indicated that their ESOP had been formed to transfer majority ownership to employees. Both of these responses apparently reflect the use of ESOPs to purchase the stock of a retiring or deceased entrepreneur.

This use of ESOPs was not anticipated in the work of Kelso or in the initial ESOP legislation, but has risen to increasing prominence as the ESOP program has matured. For a retiring firm founder, divesting to an ESOP can often be an attractive alternative to allowing the firm to be swallowed up by some large multinational firm or to closing the business altogether. Such divestitures appear to be a mechanism that can enable an ESOP to acquire an unusually high percentage of the stock in its firm. The finding that one-third of the ESOPs are designed to acquire a majority of the stock in their firms is certainly one of the most surprising results of the GAO study, and it suggests that ESOPs may have a greater role to play in the future of at least some American businesses than they have heretofore.

This use of ESOPs for divestitures may become increasingly prominent within the ESOP population as the effects of the 1984 and 1986 tax laws are felt. The tax acts of 1984 and 1986 added a number of new and attractive incentives for retiring owners or their heirs to sell businesses to their employees. DEFRA, for example, allows retiring owners to defer capital gains on stock sold to an ESOP, provided that the transaction leaves the ESOP with 30 percent or more of the company's stock. In addition, ESOPs that acquire the stock of a deceased owner may assume the tax liability of the decedent's estate, provided that the estate contributes stock to the ESOP worth at least as much as the tax liability assumed. Under the Tax Reform Act of 1986, the estates of deceased owners may exclude from their income 50 percent of the gains they receive from selling stock to an ESOP.

Conclusion

GAO data indicate that most ESOPs do little to increase employees' participation in the financial performance or the governance of their firms, and that they have little effect on the productivity or profitability of sponsoring firms. ESOPs are formed primarily to serve as retirement plans, to help companies reduce their taxes, and for other financial uses such as helping a retiring owner to extricate capital from a firm. Thanks to the diversity and attractiveness of these uses, ESOPs are likely to be with us for many years to come; but whether they will ever lead to substantial increases in employee involvement in more than a handful of firms remains to be seen.

References

Bloom, S.M. "Employee Ownership and Firm Performance." Ph.D. dissertation, Department of Economics, Harvard University, Cambridge, MA., 1985.

Brooks, L.D.; J.B. Henry; and D.T. Livingston. "How Profitable Are Employee Stock Ownership Plans?" *Financial Executive* (May 1982): 32–40.

Cohen, A., and M. Quarrey. "Employee Ownership Companies After the Founder Retires." *Journal of Small Business Management* (June 1986).

Conte, M., and A.S. Tannenbaum. "Employee Owned Companies: Is the Difference Measurable?" *Monthly Labor Review* 101 (1978): 23–28.

Ivancic, C., and C. Rosen. *Voting and Participation in Employee Ownership Firms.* Arlington, VA: National Center for Employee Ownership, 1986.

Kelso, L.O., and M.J. Adler. *The Capitalist Manifesto.* New York: Random House, 1958.

———. *The New Capitalists: A Proposal to Free Economic Growth from the Slavery of Savings.* New York: Random House, 1961.

Kelso, L.O., and P. Hetter. *How to Turn Eighty Million Workers into Capitalists on Borrowed Money.* New York: Random House, 1967.

Kelso, L.O., and P.H. Kelso. *Democracy and Economic Power Extending the ESOP Revolution.* Cambridge, MA: Ballinger, 1986.

Livingston, D.T., and J.B. Henry. "The Effects of Employee Stock Ownership Plans on Corporate Profits." *Journal of Risk and Insurance* 47 (September 1980): 491–505.

Marsh, T.R., and D.E. McAllister. "ESOPs Tables: A Survey of Companies with Employee Stock Ownership Plans." *Journal of Corporation Law* 6 (Spring 1981): 551–623.

Quarrey, M. *Employee Ownership and Corporate Performance.* Arlington, VA: National Center for Employee Ownership, 1986.

Rosen, C., and K. Klein. "Job-Creating Performance of Employee-Owned Firms." *Monthly Labor Review* 106 (August 1983): 15–19.

Rosen, C.; K. Klein; and K. Young. *Employee Ownership in America: The Equity Solution.* Lexington, MA: Lexington Books, 1986.

Tannenbaum, A.S.; H. Cook; and J. Lohmann. *The Relationship of Employee Ownership to the Technological Adaptiveness and Performance of Companies.* Ann Arbor, MI: Institute for Social Research, 1984.

Trachman, M. *Employee Ownership and Corporate Growth in High Technology Companies.* Arlington, VA: National Center for Employee Ownership, 1985.

U.S. General Accounting Office. *Employee Stock Ownership Plans: Interim Report on a Survey and Related Economic Trends.* Washington, DC: U.S. General Accounting Office, 1986a.

————. *Employee Stock Ownership Plans: Benefits and Costs of ESOP Tax Incentives for Broadening Stock Ownership.* Washington, DC: U.S. General Accounting Office, 1986b.

————. *Employee Stock Ownership Plans: Little Evidence of Effects on Corporate Performance.* Washington, DC: U.S. General Accounting Office, 1987.

Wagner, I., and C. Rosen. "Employee Ownership: Its Effect on Corporate Performance." *Employment Relations Today* (Spring 1985): 77–82.

Weitzman, M.L. *The Share Economy.* Cambridge, MA: Harvard University Press, 1984.

5. LABOR-MANAGEMENT RELATIONS: ESOPs IN THE TRUCKING INDUSTRY

Grant M. Davis and Norman A. Weintraub

THE U.S. TRUCKING INDUSTRY has been dramatically restructured since Congress passed the Motor Carrier Regulatory Reform Act of 1980 (Public Law 96–296). The total number of less-than-truck-load carriers (LTL) has declined precipitously, bankruptcies are increasing, and economic concentration is reaching alarming new levels. Rate discounting in the LTL industry is a pervasive practice and excess capacity remains an industry-wide problem (U.S. House, 1985).

Since the advent of "administrative deregulation" in 1977, a surprisingly large number of LTL carriers have ceased operations and departed the intercity for-hire freight market. Although a variety of reasons have been suggested for this, one significant factor was traffic diversion from existing LTL carriers to new low-cost truckload entrants who did not employ organized labor. Indeed, since administrative deregulation, over 110,000 union members employed by LTL carriers have either lost their jobs or endured lay-offs from the combined effect of economic recession and traffic diversion (U.S. House, 1984).

In terms of basic industrial relations practices, restructuring the LTL segment of trucking has resulted in the introduction of a special wage system for newly hired employees, significant modifications in the National Master Freight Agreement negotiated by the International Brotherhood of Teamsters (IBT) and the trucking companies, and development of "double-breasting" practices, under which unionized companies seek to operate through nonunionized subsidiaries or fictitious companies. One impact of deregulation on the freight industry's industrial relations has been the spread of employee stock ownership plans. Although these plans have not met with widespread success, they represent an important departure from traditional collective bargaining in this industry. Moreover, experience suggests that their effectiveness could be improved were they introduced in a timely and propitious manner.

ESOPs and Industrial Relations

Progressive industrial relations practices in virtually any industry should ideally be conceived and implemented in a fashion that facilitates attaining certain goals and objectives. Regarding trucking, goals normally would include growth, productivity, harmonious management-labor relationships, equitable wages and benefits, and profit sharing. Although carrier goals and objectives obviously may vary from company to company, the labor supply for LTL trucking is provided for and represented in the most part by one organization, i.e., the Teamsters.

ESOPs are not new (Kelso and Adler, 1958, Chapter 1) and during the past decade have been modified so as to include TRASOPs (tax credit employee stock ownership plans), ESOTs (employee stock ownership trusts), and other forms of employee stock ownership programs (Jachim, 1982, Chapter 2). While there are a number of ESOP-equity-based programs that have been used to finance leveraged buyouts or corporate takeovers, or to form capital, the primary purpose of employee stock ownership programs is to permit labor to gain an equity position in a firm (Miller, 1983). Theoretically, by gaining equity ownership, workers should be more productive, costly work stoppages should be avoided, and employee turnover should be diminished (Whyte et al., 1983, Chapter 1). In practice, however, not all ESOPs have been successful in slowing conflicts (Olson, 1982).

In terms of productivity, ESOPs implemented in some banking, manufacturing, retailing, and wholesale firms have experienced gains in productivity (Granrose et al., 1986). However, not all labor unions have endorsed such programs, because they tend to blur the traditional distinctions between labor and management; most union executives prefer quantifiable, tangible benefit packages in the form of wages rather than stock that is exposed to the vicissitudes of equity markets (Olson, 1982).

ESOPs and Trucking

ESOPs have been implemented by general freight motor carriers under the National Master Freight Agreement without the explicit approval of the IBT. The Union has not objected to employers' and local unions' efforts to establish ESOPs if these programs meet certain guidelines and have the voluntary participation of the employees. These ESOPs are not part of the negotiated agreement and have tended to be linked to voluntary programs of wage reductions. Under such voluntary programs, on the average, about 90 percent of the eligible employees have chosen to participate on a voluntary but irrevocable basis.

ESOPs were adopted by some carriers in response to three factors. First, the Motor Carrier Act of 1980 liberalized trucking entry requirements and, as a result, at least 27,000 new carriers entered the intercity for-hire trucking market. Not a single new carrier was represented by the IBT; all were truckload general commodity carriers that published mileage-based rates and required only a minuscule capital investment. Obviously, these carriers focused their hauling efforts upon volume movements that represented 45 percent of LTL carrier traffic, which was crucial for balance on back-hauls. Needless to say, by 1982, volume traffic for all LTL carriers had been diminished considerably from pre-1980 levels or eliminated.

Second, ESOPs were adopted because a substantial number of LTL carriers were experiencing serious financial difficulty by 1982 as a result of the 1981–1983 recession and traffic diversions, and because labor costs were 50 to 55 percent of total operating expenses. Several large carriers implemented strategies of nationwide market coverage, which in turn required massive capital commitments in the form of break-bulk facilities and equipment, commitments that most LTL carriers could not make. Once in place, these break-bulk facilities demand massive tonnage movements for mere break-even points in operations. During this same period, excess capacity became pervasive in the industry.

Third, a vicious rate war was precipitated in 1984 by break-bulk operations, excess capacity, economic recession, and a smaller traffic base together with monopsonistic pricing pressures from some shippers, a war from which the industry has not yet recovered (see, for instance, *Quarterly Operating Results of the Motor Common Carriers,* 1986; Proctor, 1987, p. 14). All these factors are and continue to be interrelated, but poor financial results, rate wars, and rising unemployment, together with new hire wage structures, constitute the quintessential forces behind trucking adoptions of ESOPs.

Trucking ESOPs are not primarily designed to ensure broad-based equity ownership in carriers by labor. They are meant to assist carriers to remain competitive and survive during the dramatic restructuring of trucking and to allay carrier management's concerns regarding survival and actuating ERISA provisions. While this observation may appear harsh, the ESOP decision, insofar as trucking is concerned, was not connected to any grandiose design to improve labor relations programs; it was implemented in reaction to the conditions that threatened thousands of jobs in the industry—by 1981, over 35,000 carrier employees had been terminated. And this is the principal shortcoming of trucking ESOPs adopted to date: For the most part, they have been implemented on a reactive basis, whereas to be successful, they should be implemented before financial difficulty is experienced.

Experience of the Trucking Industry

ESOPs were introduced into the trucking industry from 1977 through 1984, a period of increasing unemployment, bankruptcies, rate wars, excess capacity, and low levels of capital investment. Trucking's experience with ESOPs has been restricted to LTL general freight carriers. Several ESOPs remain in operation, one ESOP company has merged, and yet another ESOP carrier remains in a somewhat precarious financial condition. Recently released second-quarter earnings reveal, moreover, that the current rate-wars, designed by industry price leaders to increase market share, have not abated even though an antitrust case attacking the three leading carriers in the industry was filed in the spring of 1987 (*Lifschultz Fast Freight, Inc., v. Consolidated Freightways Corporation of Delaware, Yellow Freight System, Inc., and Roadway Express, Inc.,* U.S. District Court, Greenville, S.C. Division, Civil Action No. 6:87–477–17).

Table 1 shows how successful ESOPs have been in the trucking industry. The carriers that currently have ESOPs are identified among the larger and smaller Class I carriers. As seen in the table, Transcon initiated the first ESOP in 1983 with the coalescence of the IBT. The most recent plan is found at Advanced-United Expressways, which adopted its plan in 1986. P.I.E. represents the largest ESOP carrier in terms of both employment and revenues. Only Transcon is a publicly traded carrier.

Table 1 also shows that employment for the three largest ESOP carriers declined between 1979 and 1983, although the employment shift at Smith's Transfer may also have been affected by the fact that it was acquired recently by ACI through a stock-asset transaction involving ARA Services, Inc.

Columns F and G in Table 1 report operating rations—the ratio of revenue to costs—for 1979 and 1983, respectively. Supposedly, an ESOP can lower an operating ratio by 7.5 percent, but most carriers reported a very slight increase in the operating ratio during this period, and two showed a negligible decrease at best. In the first quarter of 1987, operating ratios for these three carriers were ominous: Transcon's was 104.9, Smith's was 107.5, and PIE's was 103.2. Obviously, these ratios were the result of continuing excess capacity, increased insurance cost, and the continuing rate war in the industry.

Perhaps, however, given the condition of the industry and the carriers, instead of looking for dramatic turnarounds from ESOPs, we should be content that the companies were able to survive. From this perspective, the seven ESOP carriers represented 24,522 employees in 1983, and revenues increased from $1.5 to $1.7 billion. Moreover, were it not for ESOPs, these companies might have gone under and the level of economic concentration would exceed its present high level.

Ten carriers, identified in Table 2, adopted ESOPs between 1983 and 1986 but have exited the intercity for-hire LTL general freight market. Table 2 contains operating and employment data for these ten carriers. As indicated in the table, 26,321 jobs were eliminated and revenues of $1.4 billion in 1983–1987 evaporated to be captured by existing or new carriers. In terms of employment, McLean Trucking represented 9,761 employees when it departed the market in 1986, with United Trucking Service having the smallest number of employees, 387 in 1986.

Each of the ten no-longer-active carriers depicted in Table 2 experienced deteriorating operating results between 1979 and 1983, although System 99 did post about a 5 percent improvement in its operating ratio. Without ESOPs, the financial results of these companies would have been worse. System 99, for example, would have posted an operating ratio 102.6 in 1983, not 95.6. If an ESOP can reduce an operating ratio approximately 7.5 percent annually, why did these ten carriers fail? There are three reasons: rate discounting escalated between 1979 and 1983, insurance costs increased dramatically in that period, and the ESOP stigma is a problem in marketing carrier services.

Table 3 depicts the entire spectrum of the LTL trucking field's experiences with ESOPs. In 1979, 65,093 employees were associated with 17 carriers that subsequently adopted ESOPs. By 1983, employment had declined from 65,093 to 50,843 for both active and terminated ESOP carriers. An even more revealing insight into the general LTL freight business involves the percentage of ESOP carriers in the 1983 market. For example, 2.3 percent of the Class I and II carriers represented 18.5 percent of operating revenues and 17.9 percent of total employment. By 1983, the number of ESOP carriers as a percentage of total carriers had increased to 2.8 percent, with 19.0 percent of operating revenues,

Table 1:
Motor Carriers of General Freight Under National Master Freight Agreement
Employee Stock Ownership Plans—Carriers in Active Operation: 1987

LARGEST CLASS I MOTOR CARRIERS	(A) YEAR ESOP ESTAB- LISHED	(B) PAYROLL DEDUCTION % of W-2 EARNINGS	(C) (MAXIMUM) PERCENT OF OWNERSHIP AT PROPOSED END OF PLAN 100% PARTICI- PATION
A.			
1. TRANSCON LINES, INC.	1983	12%	49%
2. P-I-E NATIONWIDE, INC.[a]	1985	12%	49%
3. SMITH'S TRANSFER CO.[b]	1986	15%	49%
TOTAL:			
B. *OTHER CLASS I MOTOR CARRIERS*			
1. DUFF TRUCK LINES[c]	1984	15%	49%
2. ADVANCE TRANSPORT CO.	1984	12%	45%
3. SUWAK TRUCKING	1985	15%	45%
4. ADVANCE-UNITED EXPRESSWAYS	1986	15%	48%
TOTAL:			
GRAND TOTAL— (7 ACTIVE CARRIERS)			

[a]1983 data sum of separate reports for Ryder Truck Lines, Inc. and Pacific Intermountain Express, Inc.
[b]ESOP for Smith's Transfer began on January 1, 1986. The carrier was being acquired by American Carriers, Inc. in late June 1987.
[c]Duration of 3½ years; stock for previous loan program. The carrier was acquired by O.K. Trucking Co. of Cincinnati in early June, 1987. We assume ESOP will be terminated.

(D) (E) NUMBER OF TOTAL COMPANY EMPLOYEES		(F) (G) OPERATING RATIOS		(H) (I) OPERATING REVENUES ($ MILLIONS)		(J) TYPE OF OWNERSHIP AND STOCK PRIOR TO ESOP
1979	1983	1979	1983	1979	1983	
4,817	3,764	98.0	96.7	$238.3	$283.7	N.Y. Stock Exchange
17,593	12,244	93.3	96.9	$963.7	$1,000.5	Was wholly owned subsidiary of IU International, Inc.
5,774	5,876	93.5	97.4	$253.3	$315.3	Was wholly owned subsidiary of ARA Holdings, Inc.
28,184	21,884			$1,445.3	$1,599.5	
1,154	933	99.4	101.9	$50.2	$53.6	Indpt. Company— No stock traded
770	976	97.1	98.5	$35.3	$58.8	Indpt. Company— No stock traded
261	206	98.8	100.2	$16.1	$14.3	Indpt. Company— No stock traded
460	523	95.2	942	$17.8	$31.7	Indpt. Company— No stock traded
2,645	2,638			$119.4	$158.4	
30,829	24,522			$1,574.7	$1,757.9	

Columns (D) through (I) Financial and Operating Statistics, 1979–1983, Motor Carrier Annual Reports, American Trucking Associations.

Duration of Plan: Usually about 5 years except Duff Truck lines (3½ years).

Source: Economics Dept., IBT, July 1987, Washington, D.C.

Table 2:
Motor Carriers of General Freight Under National Master Freight Agreement Employee Stock Ownership Plans— Carrier Terminated Operations: 1984–1987

Largest Class I Motor Carriers	(A) Year ESOP Established	(B) Year ESOP Terminated	(C) Payroll Deduction % of W-2 Earnings	(D) (E) No. of Total Company Empl's	
A.				1979	1983
1. INTERSTATE MOTOR FRT. SYSTEM	1983	1984	15%	5,536	4,478[a]
2. BRANCH MOTOR EXPRESS[b]	1984	1984	15%	3,032	2,346
3. ILLINOIS-CALIFORNIA EXPRESS (ICX)	1984	1984	15%	2,373	1,728
4. SYSTEM 99[c]	1985	1985	15%	1,962	1,162
5. COMMERCIAL LOVELACE MTR. FRT.	1983	1985	17.35%	2,467	1,000
6. CLAIRMONT TRANSFER CO.	1984	1985	12%	969	722
7. McLEAN TRUCKING CO.	1985	1986	15%	11,384	9,761
8. HALL'S MOTOR TRANSIT[e]	1985	1986	15%	4,167	3,555
9. UNITED TRUCKING SERVICE[f]	1984	1986	17%	796	387
10. MURPHY MOTOR FREIGHT	1986	1987	12%	1,578	1,182
TOTAL:				34,264	26,321

[a]1982 data.

[b]Two separate plans: Common stock of Branch Industries, Inc. for the voluntary ESOP; and common stock of Branch Industries, Inc. for settlement of unfair labor practice (ULP) case at WLRB.—Total of 49% Branch Motor Express was principal asset of Branch Industries.

[c]System 99 was never "endorsed" by IBT—carrier unilaterally implemented.

Source: Economics Dept., IBT, July, 1987, Washington, D.C.

(F) Operating	(G) Ratios	(H) (I) Operating Revenues ($ Millions)		(J) Maximum Percent of Ownership at Proposed End of Plan	(K) Type of Ownership and Stock of Carrier Prior to ESOP
1979	1983	1979	1983		
95.6[a]	103.5[a]	$232.9	$226.7[a]	49%	Indpt. carrier (O-T-C) market was wholly owned subsidiary of Fuqua Ind.
99.4	104.3	$135.4	$120.5	49%	Indpt. company—American Stock Exchange Branch Motor—a subsidiary
99.4[a]	101.9[a]	$108.9	$94.6[a]	100%[d]	Indpt. company—No Stock traded (empl. owned)
100.4	95.6	$88.0	$67.6	40%	Indpt. company—No stock traded
102.1	105.0	$98.3	$56.2	50.01%	Wholly owned subsidiary of Banner Indust. Inc. (N.Y. Stock Exchange)
98.2	104.4	$43.1	$43.6	49%	Indpt. company—No stock traded
100.9	101.2	$540.1	$519.0	45%	Owned by Meridian Express, Inc. (holding company for foreign interests)
95.6	103.5	$199.3	$193.4	40%	Wholly owned subsidiary of Tiger International
100.0	102.2	$56.4	$30.6	49%	Indpt. company—No stock traded
98.6	99.5	$77.5	$91.9	49%	Principal asset of MRFY, Inc.
		$1,579.9	$1,444.1		

Carrier had implemented various loan type programs and stock plans during 1981–84.

[d]With prior Stock Purchase Plan carrier would have been 100% employee owned.

[e]Hall's declared Chapter XI in March, 1986. The carrier terminated all operations except intrastate Pennsylvania with few employees left working.

[f]Plan established while company was in Chapter XI proceedings.

Source: Economics Dept., IBT, July, 1987, Washington, D.C.

Table 3:
Motor Carriers of General Freight Under NMFA Employee Stock Ownership Plans
Active and Terminated Carriers as of July 17, 1987, Summary

		NUMBER OF CARRIERS	OPERATING REVENUES (in millions)		NUMBER OF EMPLOYEES	
			1979	1983	1979	1983
Active Carriers		7	$1,574.7	$1,757.9	30,829	24,522
Terminated Carriers		10	$1,579.9	$1,444.1	34,264	26,321[a]
Total with ESOPs	1979	17	$3,154.6	$3,202.0	65,093	50,843
Total Class I & II I.C.C. Regulated Gen'l Freight Crrs.		728	$17,052.8	$16,845.0	364,364	254,063
Total with ESOPs Crrs.	1983	617				
Total with ESOPs as Percent of Total for Class I & II	1979	2.3%	18.5%	19.0%	17.9%	20.7%
I.C.C. Regulated General Freight Carriers	1983	2.8%				

[a]1982 data for Interstate Motor Freight (IMFS) and ICX.

Source: Financial and Operating Statistics, Motor Carrier Annual Reports, American Trucking Association.

and 20.7 percent of *total* employment. In short, the number of carriers, revenues, and employment falling under ESOPs increased between 1979 and 1983.

Summary and Conclusions

As can be seen, ESOPs offered to both labor and management in the trucking industry the prospects of more harmonious labor relations and greater productivity from the unionized segment of the work force.

Trucking has had two responses to the dramatic increases in bankruptcies brought about by recession, restructuring, rate wars, excess capacity, insurance problems, and traffic diversions. On the one hand, new-hire wage systems with their attendant long-term problems were implemented and accepted during the last National Master Freight Agreement. On the other, ESOPs were instituted to save jobs and permit participating carriers to remain in the intercity freight market, although many have failed because they were instituted on a reactive rather than a proactive basis.

However, ESOPs can also be effective, as shown by the fact that they constituted 20.7 percent of the Class I and II employment in 1983 and 19 percent of intercity revenues. And it is important to note that although ten ESOP carriers have failed, another underwent a merger to become part of the fifth largest truckline in the U.S. market. Therefore, in terms of maintaining employment and assets, ESOPs can be successful.

Will the number of ESOPs increase in the future? The answer is probably yes for several reasons. First, the economic environment in trucking remains hostile. Second, size economies exist in trucking, and mergers will probably increase in the future. Third, serious economic concentration questions that exist will encourage a certain level of competitiveness. Fourth, and more important, employee participation in equity ownership is a desirable social goal, and benefits ranging from capital formation to increased productivity are associated with ESOPs. Fifth, ESOP stigmas will diminish, if not disappear over time, when the private sector's overall experience with ESOPs becomes better known. Last, proactive ESOPs will be assured a higher probability of success when used in conjunction with long-range company goals.

Up to now ESOPs have been used in the trucking industry entirely for survival, having been introduced when the industry was already depressed and the fate of many firms was sealed. However, such employee stock ownership plans have the potential to be an integral part of any meaningful long-term industrial relations program.

References

"Corporate Performance Found Higher Under Employee Ownership." *Daily Labor Report* (October 1, 1986): A-13.

Employee Stock Ownership Association. *Influence Worker Motivation and Productivity Survey Finds.* Washington, DC: Employee Stock Ownership Association, 1985.

Granrose, C.S.; E. Applebaum; and V. Singh. "Saving Jobs Through Worker Buyouts." In B. D. Dennis, ed. *Proceedings of the Thirty-eighth Annual Meeting of the Industrial Relations Research Association.* Madison, WI: Industrial Relations Research Association, 1986.

Jachim, T.C. *Employee Stock Ownership and Related Plans.* Westport, CT: Quorum Books, 1982.

Kelso, L.O., and M.J. Adler. *The Capitalist Manifesto.* Westport, CT: Greenwood Press, 1958.

Klein, M.W. *Five Years After the Motor Carrier Act of 1980: Motor Carrier Failures and Successes.* Washington, DC: U.S. Department of Transportation, Office of Regulatory Affairs, September 1985.

Miller, J.J. "ESOPs, TRASOPS, and PAYSOPs: A Guide for the Perplexed." *Management Review* 72 (1983): 40–43.

Olson, D.G. "Union Experiences with Worker Ownership: Legal and Practical Issues Raised by ESOP's, TRASOP's, Stock Purchases and Cooperatives." *Wisconsin Law Review* (1982): 804–806.

Proctor, O. "ABC Leader Says Carrier Struggling." *Arkansas Democrat* (May 14, 1987): 14.

Quarterly Operating Results of the Motor Common Carriers of General Freight. Alexandria, VA: Economic Research Committee, 1986.

"Rapid Growth in Employee Ownership Causing Close Scrutiny, Conference Told." *Daily Labor Report* (May 16, 1985): A-4.

Whyte, W.F.; T. Hammer; C. Meek; R. Nelson; and R. Stern. *Worker Participation and Ownership: Cooperative Strategies for Strengthening Local Economies.* Ithaca, NY: Industrial Labor Relations Press/Cornell University, 1983.

6. GAIN SHARING AND PROFIT SHARING AS STRATEGIC CONSIDERATIONS

George T. Milkovich

THERE IS ONE THING ABOUT WHICH professors and professionals in industrial relations can be absolutely certain: concepts and techniques recycle. Profit and gain sharing are cases in point.* Both have long histories, and the arguments advanced by advocates and skeptics have a historic ring.

Systematic historical data on the use of these techniques are difficult to obtain. In 1916, a Bureau of Labor Statistics survey of manufacturing firms reported sixty profit-sharing plans in use (Bureau of Labor Statistics, 1920). The National Industrial Conference Board found 134 profit-sharing plans to describe in 1934 (National Industrial Conference Board, 1934, 1937). More recently, the Bureau of Labor Statistics survey (1984) of 195 employers reported that 19 percent used profit sharing and 2 percent used some form of gain sharing (such as Scanlon or Improshare). The American Productivity Center's survey of 1,600 firms reported that 32 percent used profit sharing and 13 percent used gain sharing (O'Dell and McAdams, 1978). Mitchell & Broderick's (1987) survey of 545 firms reported that about 50 percent used profit sharing and only 6 percent used gain sharing.**

Data aside, the current renewed interest in gain sharing is

---

*For convenience, the term gain sharing will be used in this paper to refer to all forms of variable compensation, including profit sharing. Distinctions among the various techniques will be used to report specific data or develop a point. In the compensation field, gain sharing and profit sharing are treated as two related but distinct techniques. Gain sharing usually refers to group-based incentives in which the bonus payment is determined by comparing the group's actual performance against a predetermined standard. Standards may be defined as costs, quality, quantity, safety, absenteeism, and so on. Profit sharing extends beyond work groups to include all employees in a profit center or an organization. Some threshold level of profits is the standard with profit sharing.

**Differences in results among the American Productivity Center (1987) and Mitchell and Broderick (1987) surveys are probably attributable to sample differences. Mitchell & Broderick relied heavily on firms which file IRS Form 5500, required if deferred compensation is used. The APC relied on American Compensation Association membership, a much broader cross section of U.S. firms.

reflected in the attention the topic receives at professional meetings, in journals, and in the business press.

Advocates of gain sharing assert that sharing financial gains with employees accomplishes several things. Among these are improved employee morale, which enhances loyalty and commitment (Shultz and McKersie, 1973; Bullock and Lawler, 1984); increased flow of innovative ideas from employees (Doyle, 1983); and contribution to more efficient operations and the organization's financial success (Lesieur, 1958; Metzger, 1975; O'Dell, 1984). In addition, during business downturns pay increases which are contingent on profits and/or productivity buffer the pressures to reduce employment levels. In conventional pay plans (such as merit or across the board), pay raises increase base pay. Wages are a fixed cost, at least in the short run. With gain sharing, a portion of the pay increase becomes variable. Thus, making pay increases contingent on profits and efficient operations can reduce pressures to cut employment levels during economic downturns. In practice, once these plans are implemented, managers do not have a choice of substituting reduced pay increases for employment. With gain sharing, pay increases are automatically reduced during times of poor economic performance. If gain sharing and employment were actually substitutes, a choice between the two options would exist at the point of implementation as well as in the decision to adopt gain sharing.

The variability of pay increases under gain sharing is a two-edged sword; the uncertainty for employees inherent in these plans has long been a major concern. Without gains or profits to share, variable plans are in reality risk- and loss-sharing programs. This is not a recent argument. In 1939, John L. Lewis, CIO president, labeled profit sharing a "delusionary snare" for employees. The variability in bonus payments, a central feature of these plans, creates uncertainty and threatens employees' financial well-being. Income security for employees, the criticism goes, depends on stable rather than variable income.

Other common concerns raised by skeptics include: (1) establishing acceptable performance standards, (2) changing those standards in response to new work design and technological improvements, and (3) employees' vulnerability to the vagaries of management decision making (such as new product designs or capital investment decisions) which bear directly on the financial performance of the business.

Agreement does exist on one feature of variable pay programs: these techniques do not operate in a vacuum. They are part of the broader philosophy underlying the nature of the employment relationship. The purpose of this paper is to reflect and elaborate on a point to which all parties seem to agree: that gain sharing and other variable pay techniques are part of an overall pattern of human resource policies and practices. Whatever one's perspective—be it as a researcher, manager, union official, or policy analyst—variable pay techniques, to be properly understood, need to be placed in the overall context of human resource policies and practices.

Gain Sharing Research: A Brief Review

From a research perspective, gain sharing is a set of practices in need of research and in search of theory. The literature is dominated by descriptions of various plans and prescriptions on how and when to use them. The rhetoric is mainly by advocates. Hammer (1987) argues that what is missing is an understanding of (1) the effects of gain-sharing plans, (2) the conditions under which these effects are most likely and least likely to occur, and (3) why the plans do or do not work. Answers to these three questions are provided in the extensive literature on gain sharing. But readers need to be aware that the answers are typically based on personal experience or beliefs; answers based on more systematic study are harder to find.

Few theories incorporate gain sharing, and research is not directed to search for answers to these three questions. However, both economic and psychological models are relevant. According to Hammer (1987), psychologists feel that the effects of making pay contingent on performance are well understood through learning theory and in existing models of employee motivation (Campbell and Pritchard, 1978). However, Hammer points out that gain sharing goes beyond the individual subjective utility calculations assumed in these models. Gain sharing is based on assumptions about the behavior of groups as well as individuals. Very little is known about work group behaviors, their motivations, and their effects on individual employees.

Economic models do focus on explaining observed differences in earnings and occupational attainment as well as the effects that differences have on workers' behavior. Occupational mobility, decisions to invest in training and education, and decisions to join and/or leave firms are examples of behaviors of interest in economic research. Some studies of the effects of various human resource policies and practices on the financial performance of firms have begun to appear (Ehrenberg and Milkovich, 1987).

Much of the compensation related work has focused on studying the relationships between executive pay plans and the firm's financial and market performance (Larcker, 1983; Murphy, 1985, 1986; Gomez-Mejia and Tosi, 1987). However, most of this work overlooks work groups or teams as meaningful units of analysis (Milkovich and Rabin, 1988).

Theory development may seem irrelevant to those faced with making decisions and negotiating contracts. But adequate answers to the three issues posed above are necessary, and the theories we apply to human resource management determine what we look for and how we interpret what we see, and make apparent what we do not see. Existing economic and psychological theories seldom incorporate the influence of groups and therefore the effects of gain sharing on employees or firms.

Even absent theoretical development, there is a body of research on gain sharing. It has come in three waves. The first originated at Massachusetts Institute of Technology with its historical connections to proponents such as Scanlon and Lesieur, and at Michigan State and Scanlon Plan Associates (Lesieur, 1958; Ruh, Wallace, and Frost, 1973). Beyond dissertations and technical reports, little of this work has been published. The research focuses on the Scanlon Plan, and reports that introduction of a Scanlon Plan initially increases employee suggestions for work improvements, reduces costs, improves quality, and fosters a more cooperative relationship between employees and management.

A second wave of research on gain sharing came from two surveys conducted in the early 1980s. A New York Stock Exchange (NYSE) survey revealed that approximately 15 percent of all U.S. companies with 500 or more employees had some form of productivity sharing plan; more than 70 percent of these firms reported that gain sharing led to improved productivity. Based on the *option* data of this type, the NYSE Office of Economic Research concluded that "on the basis of the *evidence and the theory*, it appears that gain sharing can play an important role in motivating people to be more productive" (emphasis added).

The other survey, a GAO Report, concluded that "the results of productivity sharing plans suggest that these plans offer a viable method of enhancing productivity at the firm level." This conclusion was based on information obtained from interviews with thirty-six firms. Of these, only twenty-four provided some financial data, only nine indicated that they made *any* formal assessment of these plans, and only four of these could document their analyses. Nevertheless, the oft-quoted GAO results are that gain sharing improved performance by 17.3 percent at thirteen firms with sales less than 100 million and by 16.4 percent in the 11 firms with sales of 100 million or greater. Since the results are based on interviews with adopters of these plans, they are open to some question.

The third wave involved a series of more recent studies on gain sharing which again focused primarily on Scanlon Plans. Bullock and Lawler (1984) reviewed thirty-three case studies to identify three factors which they hypothesized to influence gain-sharing plan success: (1) structural factors (measurement standards, eligibility, bonus share), (2) implementation factors (use of consultants, employee involvement in design and implementation), and (3) situational factors (plant size, union status). They concluded that the bonuses were granted based on performance improvement (no detailed explanation provided), a high degree of employee participation in planning was involved, and plant size did not seem to matter. Bullock and Lawler stated that over half of these cases reported tangible results of benefit to the employer. However, any differences regarding the structural, implementation, and situational properties of successful versus unsuccessful cases were not observed.

Schuster (1983a, 1984a, 1984b), in the most extensive studies of gain sharing plans, examined nine Scanlon, seven Rucker and eight Improshare plans based on monthly productivity, employment, absenteeism, and turnover data over a five-year period. Twenty-eight facilities were included. About half of the sites with data available showed significant improvements in productivity (output per employee) immediately following the plan's introduction. These improvements occurred more often in sites with plant-wide rather than team-based bonuses, causing Schuster to observe that plant-wide bonuses are preferable because of potential inequities which arise from differences in team bonuses. Schuster also suggested that unsuccessful programs tended to have (1) infrequent bonus payments, (2) management that attempted to adjust the standards and bonus formulas without employee participation, and (3) absence of union-management cooperation.

With the exception of Schuster's studies, most of the earlier research is rather poorly designed, and the statistical analysis reported is not adequate to judge the appropriateness of the conclusions drawn. A cautious conclusion is that gain sharing is associated with productivity improvements. This is based on Schuster's work and the positive halo reflecting from the other studies. However, other factors could as easily account for the results. These include changes in work design, introduction of new technologies, improved hiring and training practices, differences in base pay, and other characteristics which are part of any firm's broader approach to compensating and managing human resources. Little useful information about the other human resource policies and practices or the total compensation received by employees was reported in the research.

Gain Sharing and Human Resource Strategies

Gain sharing is often prescribed under two very divergent approaches to managing human resources. (Discussion of various prototypical human resource strategies relies heavily on recent work by Dyer and Holder, 1988.) The first, labeled a "high commitment" or "high involvement" strategy, has been the focus of much rhetoric in industrial relations (Lawler, 1986). A high commitment strategy emphasizes mutual trust between employees and managers, extensive employee participation in decision making, and an open management style which includes sharing detailed financial and operations data (Walton, 1985; Lawler, 1986).

The philosophical foundation of the high commitment strategy lies in the human relations movement (Likert, 1961), participative management (McGregory, 1960), industrial democracy (Kochan, Katz, and McKersie, 1986), and egalitarian organization cultures (Lawler, 1986). Personnel practices in this approach include job enlargement and enrichment, heavy investment in semiautonomous work groups and self-management work teams, flexitime, and a high degree of communications and information sharing. Direct supervision is replaced by facilitation. Control of employee behaviors is accomplished primarily through peer pressure rather than supervisory and hierarchically derived directives.

The pay practices prescribed under the high commitment strategy are intended to support the above characteristics. These include (1) base pay determined by the work-related skills or knowledge employees possess (for example, knowledge-based pay for factory workers, maturity curves for engineers and scientists); and (2) variable pay plans consistent with the importance of work teams, peer relationships, and the awareness of and commitment to the firm's financial success (for example, gain and profit sharing). Pay schemes that emphasize individual employee contributions and performance (merit increases, individual-based incentives) are deemphasized, as are practices typically used to determine base pay on narrow job classification. For example, job evaluation is replaced by skill evaluation procedures.

The approach followed at Borg Warner exemplifies this high commitment strategy. Borg Warner recently installed a pay plan consistent with a high commitment strategy. The facility, which assembles drive chains for transmissions, is organized into semiautonomous work teams with six to eight employees on each team. Base pay is determined by the work-related skills that each employee can demonstrate, according to the highest skill each possesses rather than the job he or she performs. Employees perform any tasks on the team for which they are qualified. The key is that base pay is linked to their highest certified skill rather than the tasks or jobs performed. Thus, these plans increase work-force flexibility and issues of working "out of job classification" do not arise. This flexibility in turn can reduce the employment levels required for given production levels.

In addition to base pay determined by skill, Borg Warner employees' pay has two additional components. Quarterly gain-sharing bonuses are based on each team's performance and a company-wide profit sharing with bonuses paid as a percent of each employee's base pay.

The Borg Warner compensation plan adheres to the prescriptions of a high commitment strategy: (1) work force flexibility and new skill acquisition are recognized through skill-based plans; (2) teamwork, peer supervision, and team performance are supported through gain-sharing plans; and (3) commitment and sensitivity to corporate financial performance are supported through profit sharing.

Another approach to managing human resources that also prescribes gain sharing has been labeled by Dyer and Holder (1988) as the "inducement strategy." It aims to insure high levels of employee performance through reliable work behaviors and low-cost production. Perhaps best characterized as the "carrot and stick" approach, its philosophic origin lies in scientific management and assumptions about "economic man."

Inducement strategies may be used by firms that compete by becoming the lowest cost producer with a quality product; the focus is on cost minimization. High levels of control over both product quality and employee work behaviors are required. Few resources are directed toward developing employee skills beyond those required on current jobs. The emphasis seems to be on operating the existing technology as efficiently as possible; there may be little interest in research and development beyond engineering improvements in current operations.

Variable compensation is the inducer or "carrot" prescribed by this strategy. Gain sharing, individual incentives (piece rates, performance bonuses), and profit sharing are all common techniques. Sizable pay increases are contingent on high performance;

high performance is defined for individual employees (performance ratings linked to individual bonuses) as well as team performance (gain sharing) and the performance of the entire firm (profit sharing).

At Lincoln Electric, for example, individual incentives have been installed for every production job as well as for the sales force (commissions). All support staff and management are on a conventional merit pay plan. Profit sharing, for which all employees are eligible, is not allocated to employees according to their earnings. Rather, profit sharing bonuses are based on each employee's performance rating. So even with a group-based incentive (corporate profits), individual bonuses are allocated according to individual performance. Bonuses at Lincoln Electric typically equal or exceed regular pay; total earnings of over $40,000 for factory employees are common.

The emphasis on individual versus group behaviors is one difference in the inducement and commitment strategies. While both may use profit sharing in an attempt to link employees to the welfare of the firm, the commitment strategy does so based on individual earnings (determined by skill or job levels) while the inducement strategy does so through individual performance ratings.

Other human resource strategies do not place the same emphasis on variable pay. Dyer and Holder (1988) and Foulkes (1986) point out that firms such as 3M, IBM, Hewlett Packard, and Eli Lilly reserve variable compensation for selected employee groups such as executives, the sales force, and top-level managers. Dyer and Holder (1988) characterize these firms as following an "investment strategy" to manage their human resources. Respect for the individual, personal growth, internal equity and justice, and high performance expectations are emphasized. High achievers (high school and college grade point averages used as hiring standards), employee competence (large expenditures on training and development), and work force flexibility through retraining and redeployment are prescribed by this strategy. Rather than following the participation-facilitation emphasized in the high commitment strategy, an investment strategy focuses on closer control and performance standards.

A compensation plan using this strategy may include base pay determined by the salary paid for particular jobs (job evaluation or straight time wages), and individual performance-based increases (performance ratings, merit increases, or merit awards). Variable pay such as profit sharing and performance bonuses based on corporate financial performance is typically limited to higher-level managers whose decisions directly affect corporate performance. However, in some firms, all employees participate in profit sharing.

The conclusion to be drawn from the foregoing is that gain sharing is embedded in the overall nature of the employment relationship. Many successful firms follow very diverse approaches to managing their human resources. Gain sharing is a dominant feature in some of these approaches, but not in others. Gain sharing plans themselves are diverse and employed for various ends. Further, it is important to note that the various human resource strategies referred to above are drawn from experience and case studies rather than empirical analysis.

The various human resource strategies discussed above do not exist in isolation. They are responses to experienced and anticipated pressures in the firm's external and internal environment. Economic pressures, legislative and regulatory directives, technological imperatives for work design and organization structures, union and employee expectations and even fads which sweep through management all effect the patterns of policies and practices which constitute human resource strategies.

Gain Sharing and the Compensation System

Gain sharing is part of the exchange between employees and employers. The nature of the exchange may be formulated through collective bargaining or it may be informal and implied, but an exchange occurs. Service and effort are rendered in exchange for returns. These returns include training, experience, status, and self-esteem; however, compensation occupies a dominant place. Consequently, to understand gain sharing and its possible effects also requires an understanding of its position in the total compensation system. Gain sharing is related to two basic compensation policy decisions: competitiveness in the market and internal equity within the pay structure.

Competitiveness in External Markets

The first policy choice, the degree of competitiveness, refers to positioning a firm's compensation relative to its competitors. Leading, meeting, and following competition are the conventional options (Milkovich and Newman, 1987). However, experience suggests that the choice is more complex, particularly with firms using gain-sharing plans.

The mix of different pay forms offered (base pay, individual incentives, gain sharing, profit sharing, benefits, and so on) affects the firm's pay posture relative to competitors. The use of gain sharing or merit bonuses (which do not roll into base pay) rather than merit increases (which do roll into base pay) give different signals in the market. For example, in an effort to control labor costs and link pay increases to performance, AT&T replaced merit increases with merit "awards." These awards do not roll into base pay. IBM, on the other hand, retains the more conventional form of merit increases. If both these firms make equivalent dollar offers to college graduates, the difference in their forms of pay seems likely to establish different competitive positions.

The point is that the risk-return trade-off inherent in the various forms of pay signals both applicants and current employees, and presumably affects their behaviors. Consider the pay plan of two firms, Lincoln Electric and another hypothetical firm. Both plans offer employees the opportunity to earn $40,000. The Lincoln Electric plan has a base of $20,000 and the potential to double that base via gain sharing. The other firm offers a $25,000 base with the potential to earn $15,000 through gain sharing. Whether the two plans have equivalent competitive positions depends on the risk-return trade-offs for prospective employees. Lincoln Electric seems to be signaling a riskier opportunity, but this depends on the probability of receiving the bonuses. The hypothetical firm's offer of $25,000 base is a certainty, but the likelihood of earning the $15,000 bonus needs to be considered, too. Perhaps more risk-averse individuals will choose one firm over the other. But determining which offer is less risky depends on the likelihood of receiving the bonus and the size of the bonus plus the base pay.

Obviously, the greater the proportion of total pay linked to gain sharing, the less income security an employee has. Japanese employees typically receive between 20 and 60 percent of their total compensation as gain-sharing bonuses. How difference in uncertainty of earnings affects employee behaviors such as the decision to join, to leave, to work smarter, or to unionize is based only on conjecture. Common sense suggests that a high base coupled with a high probability of earning a large bonus will be very appealing. The effects of different permutations of these factors are not well understood.

In addition to affecting employee work behavior, the risk-return trade-off of gain sharing affects the competitiveness of a firm's pay. To understand these effects, an offer of the opportunity to share financial gains needs to be considered in the context of the level of the base pay, the likelihood of sharing in the gains or losses, the mix of other forms in the pay system, and the offers of other firms in the market. Similarly, a tax policy designed to encourage gain sharing through preferential tax treatment would need to consider the compensation system in toto. Firms following an investment human resource strategy that does not emphasize gain sharing may be disadvantaged compared to firms following high commitment or inducement strategies under tax policies which favor variable compensation. In addition, the possibility of substitutions between gain sharing and investments in employee training or other personnel policies needs to be examined.

Internal Equity and Pay Differentials

The nature of the internal pay structure is another policy choice faced in compensation. It involves pay differentials among jobs, occupations, and skill levels within organizations. The focus of current interest regarding internal pay structures includes approaches for reducing the number of job classifications and pay levels, replacing rigid work rules associated with detailed job descriptions, and remedying pay equity concerns of women and minority employees.

Bonuses paid under gain sharing may also create differentials. By design, differential gains experienced by different work teams or among various facilities will yield differential bonus payments. For example, the Owatonna Tool Company, which manufactures hydraulic tools for automotive repair, organizes its plants into semiautonomous teams of six to eight employees. Each team is responsible for assembling specific product lines, and each has its own performance standards. Each team member receives a base wage based on the skills required to perform a set of tasks. Team bonuses are determined by comparison of the team's actual performance per quarter against a standard which includes production, quality, and safety factors.

Bonus differentials are common among the teams. Some portion of the bonus differences is attributable to factors directly under the team's control, but a portion is also attributable to difference in product lines, tolerances specified by customers, and the abilities of team members to insure that all its members are "pulling together." Some teams have had the opportunity through attrition to hire new members; others have not. The effect of these bonus differentials on each team's spirit, trust, openness, or other factors considered important under a high commitment strategy has not been systematically examined. It would seem that gain-sharing plans which create differentials among teams and/or subunits would have a different effect on employees from those plans that do not. Emphasis on egalitarianism and internal equity creates pressure to insure that all teams have equal opportunities to share in gains. This ideal is often difficult to attain. Different products, different skill compositions, and different machinery are commonplace occurrences among teams within single facilities. Owatonna Tool has a steering committee that consists of a member from each team. The committee attempts to balance factors among the various teams. However, some of the factors which create differences are simply part of the situation and are difficult to adjust.

Concluding Observations

Understanding gain sharing requires understanding the broader patterns of human resource policies and practices within which gain sharing operates. Managers, union officials, and employees all need to recognize that adopting gain-sharing schemes without consideration of other pay practices and the firm's overall approach to employee relations is shortsighted. Analysts contemplating policy recommendations to legislative bodies also need to recognize this broader context in which gain sharing plays a part. Many successful firms adopt human resource strategies in which gain sharing simply does not make sense. Researchers need to develop models that include many of the factors discussed in this paper. Attempting to understand gain sharing through many existing models limits what we think is relevant and how we interpret what we see. The patterns of human resource policies as well as the business strategies and external conditions in which the firm operates need to be included in any examination.

References

Bullock, R.J., and E.E. Lawler. "Gain Sharing: A Few Questions, and Fewer Answers." *Human Resource Management* 23 (1984): 23–40.
Bureau of National Affairs, Inc. *Productivity Improvement Programs.* Washington, DC: Bureau of National Affairs, Personnel Policies Forum No. 138, 1984.
Campbell, J.P., and R.B. Pritchard. "Motivation Theory in Industrial and Organizational Psychology." In M.D. Dunnette, ed. *Handbook of Industrial and Organizational Psychology.* Chicago: Rand-McNally, 1976.

Doyle, R.J. *Gainsharing and Productivity.* New York: AMACOM, 1983.

Dyer, L., and G.W. Holder. "Toward a Strategic Perspective of Human Resource Management." In L. Dyer, ed. *Human Resource Management: Evolving Rules and Responsibilities, ASPA/BNA Handbook of Human Resource Management,* Vol. 1. Washington, DC: Bureau of National Affairs, 1988.

Ehrenberg, R.G., and G.T. Milkovich. "Compensation and Firm Performance." In M. Kleiner, R. Block, M. Roomkin, and S. Salsburg, eds. *Research in Personnel and Human Resources Management.* Madison, WI: Industrial Relations Research Association, 1987.

Foulkes, F.K., ed. *Strategic Human Resource Management: A Guide for Effective Practice.* Englewood Cliffs, NJ: Prentice Hall, 1986.

Hammer, T.H. "New Developments in Profit Sharing, Gainsharing and Employee Ownership." In J.P. Campbell, ed. *Individual and Group Productivity in Organizations.* San Francisco, CA: Jossey-Bass, 1987.

Hewitt Associates. 1986 Profit Sharing Survey (1985 Experience). Lincolnshire, IL: Profit Sharing Council of America and Hewitt Associates, 1986.

Kochan, T.A.; H.C. Katz; and R.B. McKersie. *The Transformation of American Industrial Relations.* New York: Basic Books, 1986.

Larcker, D. "The Association Between Performance Plan Adoption and Corporate Capital Investment." *Journal of Accounting and Economics* 5 (1983): 3–30.

Lawler, E.E. *High Involvement Management.* San Francisco, CA: Jossey-Bass, 1986.

Leonard, J.S. "Carrots and Sticks: Pay, Supervision and Turnover." Unpublished paper, March 1986.

Lesieur, F.G., ed. *The Scanlon Plan: A Frontier in Labor Management Cooperation.* Cambridge, MA: Technology Press, 1958.

Likert, R. *New Patterns of Management.* New York: McGraw-Hill, 1961.

McGregory, D. *The Human Side of Enterprise.* New York: McGraw-Hill, 1960.

Metzger, B.L. *Profit Sharing in 38 Large Companies,* Vols. 1 and 2. Evanston, IL: Profit Sharing Research Fund, 1975 and 1978.

Milkovich, G.T. "A Strategic Perspective in Compensation Management." In G. Ferris and K. Rowland, eds. *Research in Human Resources Management.* Greenwich, CT: JAI Press. 1988.

Milkovich, G.T., and J. Newman. *Compensation,* 2nd ed. Plano, TX: Business Publications, Inc., 1987.

Mitchell, D.J.B., and R.F. Broderick. "Flexible Pay Systems in the American Context: History, Policy, Research and Implications." Unpublished paper, June 1987.

Murphy, K. "Corporate Performance and Managerial Remuneration: An Empirical Analysis." *Journal of Accounting and Economics* 7 (1985): 11–42.

National Industrial Conference Board. *Profit Sharing.* New York: National Industrial Conference Board, 1934.

National Industrial Conference Board. *Profit Sharing and Other Supplemen-*

tary-Compensation Plans Covering Wage Earners. New York: National Industrial Conference Board, 1937.

O'Dell, C.S. *Gainsharing, Involvement, Incentives and Productivity.* New York: American Management Association, 1981.

Ruh, R.A.; R.L. Wallace; and C.F. Frost. "Management Attitudes and the Scanlon Plan." *Industrial Relations* 12 (1973): 282–288.

Schuster, M.H. "The Impact of Union-Management Cooperation on Productivity and Employment." *Industrial and Labor Relations Review* 36 (1983a): 415–430.

Schuster, M.H. "Forty Years of Scanlon Plan Research: A Review of the Descriptive and Empirical Literature." In Colin Crouch and Frank Heller, eds. *International Yearbook of Organizational Democracy* 1 (1983b): 53–71.

Schuster, M.H. "The Scanlon Plan: A Longitudinal Analysis." *Journal of Applied Behavioral Science* 20 (1984a): 23–28.

Schuster, M.H. "Union-Management Cooperation: Structure, Process and Impact." Kalamazoo, MI: W.E. Upjohn Institute, 1984b.

Schultz, G., and R.B. McKersie. "Participation-Achievement-Reward Systems." *Journal of Management Studies* 10 (1973): 141–161.

U.S. Bureau of Labor Statistics. "Application of the Golden Rule in Business." *Monthly Labor Review* 11 (1920): 1222–1223.

U.S. General Accounting Office. "Productivity Sharing Programs: Can They Contribute to Productivity Improvement?" Washington, DC: U.S. General Accounting Office, (1981).

Walton, R.E. "From Control to Commitment in the Workplace." *Harvard Business Review* (March-April 1985): 77–84.

White, J.K. "The Scanlon Plan: Causes and Correlates of Success." *Academy of Management Journal* 22 (1979): 292–312.

7. PAY AND PERFORMANCE IN EXECUTIVE COMPENSATION

W. Bruce Johnson

CORPORATE COMPENSATION PRACTICES are designed to attract, retain, and motivate executives and employees. But despite this common purpose, explicit and implicit compensation arrangements at all organizational levels are remarkably varied across industries and across firms within a given industry (Fox, 1980). These seemingly disparate practices have generated two areas of academic inquiry.

One area of research seeks explanation for the distinctive features of firms' compensation policies, including the mix of salary and incentive compensation, the functional form of bonus schemes and profit-sharing arrangements, the distribution of pay levels for particular job classification or experience levels, and variations in internal wage hierarchies. The goal of research in this area is to understand why, and under what circumstances, specific compensation practices are used. A second and related area of research seeks to understand how alternative compensation arrangements influence employee behavior and productivity. The intent of this research is to assess the relative efficiency of particular compensation practices as mechanisms for enhancing firm performance and shareholder wealth.

This chapter summarizes recent evidence on the relationship between compensation and corporate performance, and describes the implications of this research for gain-sharing systems. Much of what we currently know about pay and firm performance comes from studies of managerial compensation; empirical results on nonmanagerial pay and firm performance are scant and inconclusive. However, since managerial compensation arrangements and gain-sharing schemes have many features in common, the existing literature can provide a useful framework for identifying issues critical to the design of effective gain-sharing programs.

Alternative Theories of Compensation

Two aspects of employee compensation are widely accepted. First, pay levels for particular job functions are determined, in theory at

123

least, by the operation of the labor market. The labor market sets
the employee's opportunity wage, and this provides a lower bound
on the amount of total compensation that must be paid to attract
and retain that person. At the same time, the availability of other
employees with comparable experience and ability at this opportunity wage provides a constraint on the level of compensation
demanded by employees in their current jobs.

Second, while tax considerations offer at least a partial explanation for certain features of corporate compensation arrangements
(Hite and Long, 1982; Miller and Scholes, 1982), compensation
contracts are not simply tax-efficient vehicles for delivering pay to
employees. Implementation costs vary across explicit and implicit
pay schemes, and the particular compensation arrangements
employed take into account some of these costs (including
favorable tax rulings).

Although opportunity wage rates and tax regulations play an
important role in shaping the compensation policies of individual
firms, these forces cannot fully account for the variety of
compensation arrangements currently observed in business organizations. How, then, can this diversity be explained?

The literature on the economics of labor markets and the agency
theory of organization provides at least four distinct hypotheses
capable of explaining variations in firms' compensation policies.
Each hypothesis is consistent with some of the stylized facts present
in the empirical literature, and most of the existing evidence can be
interpreted within any one of these perspectives. More important,
each hypothesis provides a distinctive explanation for compensation schemes that link pay to employee productivity and/or firm
performance.

One hypothesis has its roots in efficiency wage rates, market
frictions, and property rights (Williamson, Wachter, and Harris,
1975; Rosen, 1983; Yellen, 1984). According to this hypothesis,
variations in compensation levels and internal wage hierarchies
across firms reflect differences in the extent to which labor
contributes to firm value. The production technology and internal
organization of the firm, as well as the talents and abilities of
employees, jointly determine the degree to which particular job
functions enhance firm value. At the same time, severance
agreements, employee recruiting costs, and investments that
develop firm-specific human capital (specialized skills) create
market frictions that cause significant economic benefit to arise
from enduring employment relationships. Thus, idiosyncratic
production functions and labor market frictions provide a partial

explanation for pay schedules linked to employee productivity and firm performance.

A related hypothesis proposes that compensation contracts function as mechanisms for screening and sorting among employees of differing ability levels (Spence, 1981; Harris and Holmstrom, 1982). According to this hypothesis, labor contracts are designed to attract and retain the "best" employees while providing incentives for the less able to abstain from applying or to resign. Employee ability is either unknown (except by the employee) or costly to observe, and compensation contracts are structured so that employees truthfully reveal their ability. Performance-based compensation contracts in this setting are not intended to stimulate greater effort or productivity on the part of currently employed workers; rather, these contracts simply represent a cost-effective way of screening potential employees of varying ability levels.

The third hypothesis provides a radically different explanation for performance-contingent compensation schemes. Under the signaling hypothesis (Larcker and Johnson, 1981; Raviv, 1985), employees are assumed to possess private (inside) information about the future prospects of the firm. According to this perspective, firms adopt stock option and profit-sharing plans when employees anticipate favorable share price or profit performance; thus, compensation arrangements convey information about employees' private information. The signaling hypothesis predicts that adoption of performance-based contracts will result in stock price appreciation since adoption provides a credible signal regarding firms' expected future performance. Note, however, that the pay/performance link is explained with reverse causality: Employee compensation and firm performance are correlated not because performance-based contracts encourage increased productivity and efficiency, but because those contracts are introduced when favorable prospects lie ahead.

The final hypothesis, and certainly not the least important, is that performance-based compensation plans are designed to bring the incentives of management and employees in line with those of shareholders (Holmstrom, 1979; Lazear and Rosen, 1981; Grossman and Hart, 1983). The direction of causality implied by the incentive-alignment hypothesis is clear: Compensation arrangements that reduce incentive conflicts (employee shirking, expense preference behaviors, and differences in risk attitudes and decision horizons) stimulate increased productivity and efficiency, and thus increase firm performance and shareholder wealth. Moreover, this hypothesis predicts that performance-contingent compensation plans will be introduced when other mechanisms (peer pressure, internal monitoring, and labor market discipline) are insufficient to control the conflicts of interest that arise within the firm.

Briefly then, the efficiency wage/market frictions hypothesis relies on differences in firms' production technologies, employment transactions costs, and labor markets to explain variations in compensation policies. The screening/sorting hypothesis focuses on unknown employee ability, and emphasizes the role of compensation in attracting and retaining employees. The signaling hypothesis argues that performance-contingent compensation arrangements have no impact on worker productivity but instead convey information regarding expectations about firms' future prospects. The incentive-alignment hypothesis argues that compensation policies function to reduce agency problems and that incentive pay schemes lead directly to increased firm performance and shareholder wealth. Of course, the incentive-alignment perspective is implicit in many of the arguments advanced by advocates of gain-sharing programs.

The Evidence on Managerial Compensation

Empirical research on the relationship between managerial compensation and corporate performance has focused on four broad areas: the correlation between executive pay and firm performance, the effect of accounting-based bonus contracts on managers' decisions, the impact of compensation plan adoption on shareholder wealth, and variations in managerial pay levels.

Managerial Pay and Firm Performance

Are managerial compensation contracts really designed to "pay for performance," when performance is measured by changes in shareholder wealth? The answer appears to be a qualified yes. There is a positive, statistically significant correlation between changes in management compensation and changes in shareholder wealth (Benston, 1985; Coughlan and Schmidt, 1985; Murphy, 1985, 1986). For example, one comprehensive study of managerial pay in 1,200 large corporations over ten years found that executives received pay increases of less than 1.0 percent when stockholder returns were -20.0 percent or lower; however, when stock price performance exceeded +40.0 percent, pay increases averaged about 14.0 percent (Murphy, 1985). A related study by Lambert and Larcker (1984a) found that substantial increases in firm size via acquisitions were associated with increases in real (inflation-adjusted) executive compensation relative to size and industry standards. More important, virtually all of the compensation increase went to managers who made acquisitions that also increased shareholder wealth; managers who undertook acquisitions that reduced share prices saw no increase in the relative level of real compensation.

While these studies demonstrate that managerial pay and firm performance are related, the correlation coefficients between compensation and (accounting or market) measures of corporate performance are typically small, and rather modest changes in pay occur for large changes in shareholder wealth. For example, Murphy (1985) reports that a 10 percent change in equity value of the firm is associated with only about a 2 percent increase in compensation. One explanation for the rather small correlations obtained in some studies is that executives' stock holdings and stock options were excluded from the compensation measure used by the researchers. Managers with significant stock or option positions in their companies are clearly rewarded for good performance (and penalized for bad performance) since the value of their personal holdings is tied directly to changes in shareholder wealth and the economic performance of the firm.

On the other hand, we know very little about how closely nonstock components of compensation (salary, yearly bonuses, and performance plan awards) should be correlated with annual stock price changes or accounting measures of firm performance. Using stock prices as the sole performance criterion may expose managers to excessive risks for factors beyond their control. This problem can be partially mitigated if compensation is also based on one or more nonmarket measures of firm performance (earnings per share or sales growth) that "filter out" the effects of random events on managerial pay. Hence, the absence of a strong relationship between executive compensation and shareholder wealth need not be an indication of the irrationality of corporate pay practices; small positive correlations may be consistent with optimal compensation arrangements for managers in highly cyclical industries who are exposed to large uncontrollable risks.

While there is ample evidence indicating that managerial pay and corporate performance are positively correlated, the direction of causality remains open to debate. One possibility is that certain compensation arrangements induce managers to take actions that enhance firm performance and shareholder wealth, as suggested by the incentive-alignment hypothesis. However, the pay/

performance correlation can also be explained without appealing to the notion that performance-based compensation leads to increased productivity and efficiency. Thus, we are left with the rather perplexing problem of whether the chicken or the egg came first.

Do Compensation Contracts Alter Managerial Behavior?

This question has been addressed in a number of studies examining the effects of alternative compensation schemes on managerial decision making. This research has shown that adoption of accounting-based bonus contracts is associated with reductions in perquisite consumption (Larcker, 1984) and with increases in long-term capital investment expenditures (Larcker, 1983). One study found that the profit-sharing features of oil/gas partnership agreements partially explained differences in drilling agents' decisions regarding the curtailment of exploration (Wolfson, 1985). Several studies have shown that incentive compensation schemes, the availability of "golden parachutes," and the dependence of managers' personal wealth on stock prices influence corporate acquisition decisions and takeover resistance (Lambert and Larcker, 1984a and 1985; Benston, 1985; Lewellen, Loderer, and Rosenfeld, 1985; Walkling and Long, 1984; Tehranian, Travlos, and Waegelein, 1987).

The immediate conclusion suggested by these findings is that variations in executive compensation arrangements are related to differences in managerial behavior, although the direction of causality is again unclear. A somewhat speculative conclusion, also consistent with the empirical results of one study (Healy, 1985), is that managers behave opportunistically by manipulating the accounting numbers on which their compensation is based. These manipulations shift revenues and expenses from one period to another, and often involve rather subtle changes in operating decisions (such as delaying repair and maintenance). More visible accounting manipulations (changing depreciation methods, for example) do not appear to generate additional compensation (Healy, Kang, and Palepu, 1987).

Compensation Plans and Shareholder Wealth

Studies investigating the impact of compensation plans on shareholder wealth have demonstrated that initiation of management compensation contracts or changes in those contracts affect the stock prices of the firms involved. Here we learn that stock prices rise by about 11 percent (on average) when companies adopt bonus plans that reward short-term performance (Tehranian and Waegelein, 1985). Shareholders realize a 2 percent return when companies introduce long-term compensation plans that link managerial pay to firm performance (Brickley, Bhagat, and Lease, 1985; Larcker, 1983), and stock prices increase by 3 percent when companies adopt "golden parachute" provisions (Lambert and Larcker, 1985). In each study, common stock values not only increase when companies introduce the compensation scheme but the stock continues to trade at the new, higher level. In addition, companies that initiate managerial stock option plans exhibit reductions in the variance (risk) of common stock returns (Lambert and Larcker, 1984b).

Collectively, these studies demonstrate that executive compensation contracts are important to investors as well as managers. At the same time, these results are somewhat difficult to interpret because the share price response to compensation plan adoption reflects the market-assessed desirability of both the pay plan and any new strategy changes that are being introduced at the same time.

Managerial Pay Levels and the Labor Market

The fact that changes in compensation are correlated with changes in shareholder wealth, or that shareholder wealth increases when new compensation plans are adopted, tells us little about whether the level of executive compensation is correct, that is, whether managers are being paid more than or less than their contribution to the firm. One study (Johnson et al., 1985) found a pronounced negative stock price reaction to the "unexpected" deaths of senior corporate executives who were not the founders of their companies. This result suggests that CEOs are not overpaid relative to their contribution to shareholder wealth (not at least when compared to alternative managers available in the labor market). In a related study, Johnson, Magee, and Harris (1987) found that common stock prices increased roughly 2 percent when individuals from outside the organization were appointed to previously vacated senior executive positions. This result reinforces the conclusion that senior executives are not overpaid: Hiring a manager from the external labor market yields a net (of compensation) increase in shareholder wealth, although the source of this gain remains somewhat speculative.

According to the efficiency wage/market frictions hypothesis, variations in managerial pay levels across firms should be related to differences in managers' contributions to firm value. Johnson et al. (1985) have shown that the share price decreases which occur following an unexpected executive death are negatively correlated with the deceased manager's (former) position in the pay hierarchy relative to that of the next highest-paid executive in the firm. At the same time, the price increases that accompany external appointments to vacant managerial posts are positively correlated with the new executive's relative position in the firm's compensation hierarchy (Johnson, Magee, and Harris, 1987). Although the evidence is indirect, these results are consistent with the view that variations in internal wage hierarchies at the managerial level reflect differences in the relative contribution of managerial functions (and of the managers themselves).

A second explanation for managerial wage differentials across firms or industries can be derived from an analysis of compensation risk/reward tradeoffs. Although performance-based pay schemes can reduce conflicts of interests between managers and stockholders, they can also greatly increase executives' exposure to risk when the performance measures (for example, stock prices) are influenced by uncontrollable factors, and diversification opportunities are limited. In the absence of market frictions, managers will demand increased compensation in return for bearing additional risk. Antle and Smith (1985) have shown that the average level of total compensation (salary plus bonus plus change in the value of stockholdings) paid to executives is positively related to the riskiness of compensation. Thus, differences in compensation levels across firms can be partially attributed to differences in managers' exposure to compensation risk.

Finally, one important facet of the managerial labor market is its ability to "discipline" managers by lowering the current (and future) opportunity wage of those managers who perform poorly. This assumes, of course, that the labor market has good information about the performance of individual managers and about the impact of managerial behavior on firm value and shareholder wealth. To be fired is to face the most extreme form of labor market discipline, especially when this makes it difficult to obtain another comparable job. Coughlan and Schmidt (1985), among others, have shown that terminations are more likely to occur after decreases in shareholder wealth or periods of low earnings performance, a result consistent with labor market disciplining.

In summary, the available evidence on managerial compensation and corporate performance suggests (1) that changes in compensation are correlated with changes in firm performance; (2) that alternative incentive compensation schemes are associated with differences in managerial behaviors and decisions; (3) that stock prices (on average) increase when new compensation plans are adopted; and (4) that the distribution of managerial pay levels is related to differences in managers' contributions to firm value and to differences in the risk/return characteristics of the compensation scheme.

Evidence on Employee Compensation

With respect to nonmanagerial compensation, perhaps the single most striking feature of research on this subject is that the link between compensation policy and firm performance (or shareholder wealth) is rarely examined. Most studies of nonmanagerial compensation limit their attention to the effects of alternative compensation schemes on the behavior of individual employees or work groups, and on employee attitudes (see Ehrenberg and Milkovich's chapter in this book). We learn, for example, that pay levels are positively correlated with the size of the employee applicant queue, and are negatively correlated with employee turnover and absenteeism. Of course, firms that offer high wages in an attempt to reduce employee turnover and absenteeism may be merely substituting increases in one type of labor cost (compensation) for cost reductions elsewhere (turnover/absenteeism). Whether this strategy produces a net increase in firm value and shareholder wealth remains open to conjecture.

Interpretation of the evidence on employee incentive plans is fraught with difficulty as well. Employee pay-for-performance schemes "work" in the sense that incentive plans are associated with statistically significant increases in worker productivity, performance, employee job satisfaction, organizational commitment, and so on (Lawler, 1971). The evidence is less clear on whether pay-for-performance schemes induce temporary or relatively permanent changes in employee attitudes and behaviors, or whether the value (to shareholders) of increased productivity and efficiency exceeds the costs of implementing and monitoring individual and group incentive schemes at nonmanagerial levels of the organization.

By providing an explicit link between employee wealth and the economic fortunes of the firm as a whole, employee profit-sharing or stock ownership plans can overcome some of the limitations inherent in individual and group incentive schemes. However, profit-sharing and stock ownership plans are frequently adopted for reasons other than to serve as incentive-alignment devices that enhance worker productivity. For example, they may substitute for employee thrift or pension plans, they may facilitate leveraged buyouts or impede hostile takeover attempts, or they may be part of negotiated wage concession agreements. At the same time, the details of gain-sharing systems are remarkably diverse. Profit-sharing schemes differ in the extent to which bonuses are paid currently or are deferred, whether the bonus formula is fixed or discretionary, and whether deferred bonuses are invested in stock of the employer or in a diversified portfolio. Similarly, ESOPs vary in the extent of employees' equity participation, voting rights, and so on. These distinctive features have important implications for incentive alignment; they also add "noise" to the data and make it more difficult to draw meaningful conclusions from the available evidence.

What is that evidence? Most studies suggest that profit sharing and ESOP firms out-perform their competitors on a variety of measures: profits as a percent of net worth and revenues, sales growth, dividend rates, and so on. One recent study (Quarrey, 1986) found that ESOP companies had significant increases in sales and employment growth rates after establishing employee owner-ship plans when compared to a matched group of non-ESOP companies. However, much of the evidence on gain sharing, firm performance, and shareholder wealth remains inconclusive: the direction of causation is generally left undetermined, the samples are typically small, and the research designs are often of questionable validity. Consequently, it is unclear whether these companies do better because they adopt gain-sharing plans, or more successful companies are more likely to set up plans, or perhaps better managers are more interested in sharing profits and ownership. On the other hand, shareholders realize a 3.0 percent return when firms adopt employee stock purchase plans restricted to key managers, and a 1.5 percent return when the plan allows broad employee participation (Bhagat, Brickley, and Lease, 1985). This finding is consistent with both the signaling hypothesis and the incentive-alignment hypothesis described earlier.

In short, studies of employee compensation and firm perform-ance have clearly demonstrated that productivity gains at the individual and work-group level can be achieved through incentive compensation and gain sharing. These studies also document significant improvements in employee morale. An open question, however, is whether these productivity and performance gains contribute more to firm value than is lost through increased compensation. In other words, do individual and group incentive programs yield net economic benefits to shareholders?

Concluding Remarks

While academics enjoy the luxury of speculation and can await the arrival of definitive evidence, business professionals confront the more immediate and demanding task of restructuring corporate compensation policies to compete effectively in global markets. Gain sharing represents a potentially viable response to these competitive pressures, and the studies summarized above underscore several key issues of critical importance to the design of effective gain-sharing systems.

First, our current understanding of managerial compensation arrangements makes it abundantly clear that gain-sharing plans, as mechanisms for enhancing firms' economic performance, must be tailored to the specific characteristics and circumstances of the firm or business unit. The production technology and internal organization of the firm or business unit, its strategic objectives and stage of development, the economics of the industry and the regulatory environment, and the nature of employee labor markets jointly determine the effectiveness of particular employee incentive schemes. In light of these complexities, no single gain-sharing scheme is likely to have universal applicability. Experimentation and "fine tuning" are required to identify the circumstances under which various employee incentive schemes do or do not work. This may be an area where practice leads academic research.

Second, compensation serves to attract, retain, and motivate employees. Different elements of compensation have varying effects on these goals. For example, salary may be useful in attracting employees, but is perhaps less useful in motivating or retaining employees. Deferred incentive schemes tend to be useful in both retention and motivation. What proportion of an employee's total compensation should come from gain sharing? The optimal mix of salary and incentive compensation undoubtedly varies across firms and job functions as a consequence of production technologies, labor markets, and wage equity considerations.

Third, identifying the proper scorecard for evaluating employee performance and awarding incentive payments under gain sharing is itself a difficult task. Tradeoffs must be made between the use of productivity, cost, and profit measures of performance; between short-run or long-run performance criteria; and so on. Needless to say, an optimal scorecard for evaluating managerial performance has yet to be identified except in rather contrived settings, and we know even less about optimal scorecards at the nonmanagerial level where the link between employee productivity and firm performance is perhaps more tenuous. However, multiple performance criteria play an important role in executive compensation contracts, and thus they are likely to prove useful in gain-sharing programs as well.

Fourth, incentive compensation arrangements and stock ownership plans impose additional risks on employees because uncontrollable forces can affect the performance measure and the value of employee stock holdings. A partial solution to this problem involves the use of "relative performance" schemes where incentive compensation awards are set according to how well the firm (or business unit) performed in comparison to a competitor or peer group. This approach allows general market or macroeconomic influences and industry-specific influences to be removed from the performance measure, thereby providing a clearer indication of employees' distinctive contribution to the firm's economic performance.

There are, of course, a number of other important questions that warrant thoughtful consideration, such as how gain sharing affects the budgeting and planning process.

To conclude, studies of pay and firm performance document a variety of empirical regularities which are essential building blocks for the development of more efficient compensation packages at all levels of the organization—compensation packages that yield increases in worker productivity, firm performance, and perhaps shareholder wealth. At the same time, it is important to recognize that the potential benefits of incentive compensation generally, and gain sharing in particular, extend beyond the narrow perspective implied by the preoccupation here with shareholder wealth. Gain sharing can generate positive externalities of considerable significance (reduced turnover and unemployment, product innovations, and quality improvements) that enhance the lives of workers and enable businesses to compete effectively in today's economic environment even though these benefits are not fully captured by shareholders.

References

Antle, R. and A. Smith. "Measuring Executive Compensation: Methods and an Application." *Journal of Accounting Research* 23 (Spring 1985): 296–325.

Benston, G.J. "The Self-serving Management Hypothesis: Some Evidence." *Journal of Accounting and Economics* 7 (1985): 67–84.

Bhagat, S.; J. Brickley; and R. Lease. "Incentive Effects of Employee Stock

Purchase Plans." *Journal of Financial Economics* 8 (1985): 195–216.

Brickley, J.; S. Bhagat; and R. Lease. "The Impact of Long-range Managerial Compensation Plans on Shareholder Wealth." *Journal of Accounting and Economics* 7 (1985): 115–130.

Coughlan, A., and R. Schmidt. "Executive Compensation, Management Turnover, and Firm Performance: An Empirical Investigation." *Journal of Accounting and Economics* 7 (1985): 43–66.

Fox, H. *Top Executive Compensation.* New York: Conference Board, 1980.

Grossman, S., and O. Hart. "An Analysis of the Principal-agent Problem." *Econometrica* 51 (1983): 7–45.

Harris, M., and B. Holmstrom. "A Theory of Wage Dynamics." *Review of Economic Studies* 49 (1982): 315–333.

Healy, P. "Evidence on the Effect of Bonus Schemes on Accounting Procedure and Accrual Decisions." *Journal of Accounting and Economics* 7 (1985): 85–108.

Healy, P.; S. Kang; and K. Palepu. "The Effect of Accounting Procedure Changes on CEOs' Cash Salary and Bonus Compensation." *Journal of Accounting and Economics* 9 (1987): 7–34.

Hite, G., and M. Long. "Taxes and Executive Stock Options." *Journal of Accounting and Economics* 4 (1982): 1–14.

Holmstrom, B. "Moral Hazard and Observability." *Bell Journal of Economics* 10 (1979): 74–91.

Johnson, B.; R. Magee; N. Nagarajan; and H. Newman. "An Analysis of the Stock Price Reaction to Sudden Executive Deaths: Implications for the Managerial Labor Market." *Journal of Accounting and Economics* 7 (1985): 151–174.

Johnson, R.; R. Magee; and D. Harris. "Executive Succession, External Labor Markets and Shareholder Wealth." Northwestern University, Kellogg Graduate School of Management Working Paper, 1987.

Lambert, R., and D. Larcker. "Executive Compensation Effects of Large Corporate Acquisitions." Northwestern University, Kellogg Graduate School of Management Working Paper, 1984a.

———. "Stock Options and Managerial Incentives." Northwestern University, Kellogg Graduate School of Management Working Paper, 1984b.

———. "Golden Parachutes, Executive Decision Making, and Shareholder Wealth." *Journal of Accounting and Economics* 7 (1985): 179–204.

Larcker, D. "The Association Between Performance Plan Adoption and Corporate Capital Investment." *Journal of Accounting and Economics* 5 (1983): 3–30.

———. "Short-term Compensation Contracts, Executive Expenditure Decisions, and Corporate Performance: The Case of Commercial Banks." Northwestern University, Kellogg Graduate School of Management Working Paper, 1984.

Larcker, D., and B. Johnson. "The Adoption of Multiple-year Performance-based Executive Compensation Plans." Northwestern University, Kellogg Graduate School of Management Working Paper, 1981.

Lawler, E. *Pay and Organization Effectiveness.* New York: McGraw-Hill.

1971.

Lazear, E., and S. Rosen. "Rank-order Tournaments as Optimum Labor Contracts." *Journal of Political Economy* 89 (1981): 841–864.

Lewellen, W.; C. Loderer; and A. Rosenfeld. "Merger Decisions and Executive Stock Ownership." *Journal of Accounting and Economics* 7 (1985): 209–232.

Miller, M., and M. Scholes. "Executive Compensation, Taxes and Incentives." In W. Sharpe and C. Cootner, eds. *Financial Economics: Essays in Honor of Paul Cootner.* Englewood Cliffs, NJ: Prentice Hall, 1982.

Murphy, K. "Corporate Performance and Managerial Remuneration: An Empirical Analysis." *Journal of Accounting and Economics* 7 (1985): 11–42.

———. "Incentives, Learning and Compensation: A Theoretical and Empirical Investigation of Managerial Labor Contracts." *Rand Journal of Economics* 17 (1986): 59–76.

Quarrey, M. *Employee Ownership and Corporate Performance.* Oakland, CA: National Center for Employee Ownership, 1986.

Raviv, A. "Management Compensation and the Managerial Labor Market: An Overview." *Journal of Accounting and Economics* 7 (1985): 239–246.

Rosen, S. "Specialization and Human Capital." *Journal of Labor Economics* 1 (1983): 43–49.

Spence, M. "Signaling, Screening, and Information." In S. Rosen, ed. *Studies in Labor Economics.* Chicago: University of Chicago Press, 1981.

Tehranian, H.; N. Travlos; and J. Waegelein. "Management Compensation Contracts and Merger-induced Abnormal Returns." *Journal of Accounting Research* 25 (1987): 51–84.

Tehranian, H., and J. Waegelein. "Market Reaction to Short-term Executive Compensation Plan Adoption." *Journal of Accounting and Economics* 7 (1985): 131–144.

Walkling, R., and M. Long. "Agency Theory, Managerial Welfare, and Takeover Bid Resistance." *Rand Journal of Economics* 15 (1984): 54–68.

Williamson, O.; M. Wachter; and J. Harris. "Understanding the Employment Relation: The Analysis of Idiosyncratic Exchange." *Bell Journal of Economics* 6 (1975): 250–278.

Wolfson, M. "Empirical Evidence of Incentive Problems and Their Mitigation in Oil and Gas Tax Shelter Programs." In J. Pratt and R. Zeckhauser, eds. *Asymmetric Information, the Agency Problem, and Modern Business.* Cambridge, MA: Harvard University Press, 1985.

Yellen, J. "Efficiency Wage Models of Unemployment." *American Economic Review* 74 (1984): 200–205.

8. MACROECONOMIC IMPLICATIONS OF PAY AND PERFORMANCE: THE SHARE ECONOMY

Martin C. Weitzman

RECENTLY, THERE HAS BEEN A tremendous resurgence of interest in share arrangements generally, and in profit sharing particularly. This new interest has been manifesting itself in a variety of ways, especially in statistics concerning actual pay settlements. However, even without such numbers, we all know there is a lot more talk about gain-sharing arrangements than we have heard in a long time.

Recent Interest in Profit Sharing

Profit sharing itself is an old idea with a venerable history. There are a number of reasons for the rekindled interest of late. A major direct spur is undoubtedly coming from the fierce pressure for containing costs, or at least making them somewhat more responsive to performance, to which many previously quasi-protected industries are subjected in today's deregulated, internationally competitive environment. Another rationale for profit sharing stems from the more general idea that a properly instituted gain-sharing plan can motivate workers to cooperate more fully with management in raising productivity and increasing profitability because they have a direct stake in the outcome. And there is the idea that if society as a whole were to move toward profit sharing, it would help to soften the wicked unemployment-inflation tradeoff that bedevils current attempts of traditional macroeconomic policy to reconcile reasonably low unemployment with reasonably low inflation. This macroeconomic promise of profit sharing is what I will concentrate on here by attempting to set forth the general case briefly and informally.

One crucial fact must be emphasized. Unemployment is extraordinarily expensive, not to mention immoral. Lowering our average national unemployment rate from about 7 percent to the 4 percent level prevailing, say, in Massachusetts, would translate into an annual increase in national income of about a quarter of a trillion

137

dollars. Is it beyond us, as an economy and as a society, to create an industrial relations system that builds in stronger incentives to employ more workers and to keep them employed despite fluctuations in the economy?

One important difference exists between how someone with an economist's perspective is likely to view labor-payment systems and how someone coming from a pure industrial relations background is likely to see things. The economist tends to regard narrowly defined industrial relations as essentially concerned with the interests of two parties in the work place: management and the already employed, in-place, existing core labor force—"insider" workers, in the economist's jargon. Relatively little attention is paid to third party "outsiders"—the unemployed and those who, when they have jobs, constitute the low-seniority, untenured, last-hired, and first-fired work force. Yet industrial relations generally, and pay policies in particular, have profound effects on unemployment and inflation. Surely an industrial relations system could be crafted to preserve most of the traditional desiderata that insiders value while building in stronger incentives to employ more outsiders and to keep them employed through good and bad times.

Japanese Labor-Payment System

Japan has an unusual labor-payment system in which about one-fourth of an average worker's total compensation comes in the form of a semi-annual bonus supplement added onto base wages. It has by now been pretty firmly established that the Japanese bonus system can be viewed as a form of profit sharing, even though only about 15 percent of Japanese firms explicitly link the bonus to profitability via a prescribed formula. Statistically, Japanese bonuses can be viewed as a form of profit sharing because the ratio of bonus payments to base wages varies positively with business condition indicators, including profitability per employee.

Japan has enjoyed the lowest average unemployment rate among the major industrialized capitalist economies over the last quarter century. This comparatively outstanding employment record survives corrections for discouraged workers, relatively flexible hours, definitional differences, and so forth. Does the existence of a profit-sharing component of pay in any way help to account for the comparatively low, stable unemployment rate in Japan?

This is an easy question to ask, but a very hard one to answer. The whole Japanese system seems to promote employment, making it impossible to isolate the pure role of the bonus system. I think it is fair to say, however, that Japanese firms would have difficulty maintaining the full-employment commitment without the automatic cushion that the bonus system provides. The Japanese experience is definitely suggestive or supportive of the proposition that a profit-sharing system can be used to help promote full employment. But it would be naive to try to go far beyond such a statement at this stage.

Causes of Unemployment

What causes unemployment or slack labor markets? There is only one basic answer, but, like a coin, the answer has two sides. Side one says that unemployment is caused when firms suffer insufficient demand for their products relative to their marginal costs of production. Side two says that unemployment is caused when the firms' marginal costs of production are too high relative to the demand for their products. Sometimes it is useful to stress one side of the coin, sometimes the other. But it is always the same coin.

In either case, the key to noninflationary full employment is an economic expansion that holds down the marginal cost to the firm of acquiring more labor. Macroeconomic policy alone—the purposeful manipulation of financial aggregates—can be very powerful in achieving full employment or price stability but cannot be reliably depended upon to reconcile both simultaneously. Why? Because of the two-headed monster—"stagflation." Illusions of being able to fine tune aside, we know how to use the usual expansionary monetary and fiscal measures to decrease unemployment and increase output. We also know how to break inflation by policy-induced recessions. What we do *not* know—and this is the central economic dilemma of our time—is how *simultaneously* to reconcile reasonably full employment with reasonable price stability. To an excessive degree, expansionary policies result in too-large wage and price increases rather than in expanded employment and output.

Macroeconomic Problems

The major macroeconomic problems of our day can be traced back ultimately to the wage system of paying labor. We try to award every employed worker a predetermined piece of the income pie before it is out of the oven, before the size of the pie is even known. Our "social contract" promises workers a fixed wage independent of the health of their company, while the company chooses the employment level. This stabilizes the money income of whoever is hired, but only at the considerable cost of loading unemployment on low-seniority workers and inflation on everybody—a socially inferior risk-sharing arrangement that both diminishes and makes more variable the real income of workers as a whole. An inflexible money-wage system throws the entire burden of economic adjustment on employment and the price level. Then macroeconomic policy is called upon to do the impossible—reconcile full employment with low inflation.

A profit-sharing system in which some part of a worker's pay is tied to the firm's profitability per employee puts in place exactly the right incentives to resist unemployment and inflation. If workers were to allow some part of their pay to be more flexible by sharing profits with their company, that would improve macroeconomic performance by directly attacking the economy's central structural rigidity. The superiority of a profit-sharing system is that it has enough built-in flexibility to maintain full employment even when the economy is out of balance from some shock to the system. When part of a worker's pay is a share of profits, the company has an automatic inducement to take on more employees in good times and, what is probably more significant, to lay off fewer workers during bad times. A profit-sharing system is not antilabor and does not rely on lowering workers' pay for its beneficial effects. The key objective is not to reduce worker pay—it could even go up within reason—but to lower the base-wage component relative to the profit-sharing component. The marginal cost of labor is approximately the base wage, more or less independent of the profit-sharing component.

While it is possible to dream up unlikely counterexamples and to interpret the existing evidence perversely, the bulk of economic theory, empirical evidence, and common sense argue that widespread profit sharing will help to improve macroeconomic performance. The bottom line is that it is easy to envision situations where profit sharing helps macroeconomic performance, while it is difficult to imagine scenarios where profit sharing damages an economy, which is as much as can be claimed for any economic idea.

The Case for Profit Sharing

The British Chancellor of the Exchequer stated the case for profit sharing as follows in his 1986 annual budget speech before the House of Commons:

The problem we face in this country is not just the level of pay in relation to productivity, but also the rigidity of the pay system. If the only element of flexibility is in the numbers of people employed, then redundancies are inevitably more likely to occur. One way out of this might be to move to a system in which a significant proportion of an employee's remuneration depends directly on the company's profitability per person employed. This would not only give the work force a more direct personal interest in their company's success, as existing employee share schemes do. It would also mean that, when business is slack, companies would be under less pressure to lay men off; and by the same token they would in general be keener to take them on (*Financial Times,* 1986).

It is no mystery why profit sharing changes the employer's view. In a profit-sharing system, the young school graduate looking for work comes with an implicit message to the employer saying: "Hire me. I am reasonable. Your only absolute commitment is to pay me the base wage. That is my marginal cost to you. The profit-sharing bonus is like a variable cost, depending to some extent on how well the company is doing. So you have a built-in cushion or shock absorber if something should go wrong. You won't be under such pressure to lay off me or other workers during downswings." By contrast, the young school graduate looking for work in a wage system now comes to a potential employer with the implicit message: "Think very carefully before you hire me. I am expensive and inflexible. You will have to pay me a fixed wage independent of whether your company is doing well or poorly." Is it difficult to deduce in which situation companies might be expected to recruit new hires more eagerly and to retain them, and in which situation new hiring commitments are likely to be avoided when possible? The essence of the case for profit sharing is the basic idea that on the margin the profit-sharing firm is more willing than the wage firm to hire new workers during good times and, more importantly, to lay off fewer workers during bad times. From a social point of view, a wage system is poorly designed because it is inherently so rigid. A precise relation must exist between the wage level and the level of aggregate demand to hit exactly the full employment target without causing inflation. By contrast, a profit-sharing system is inherently much more forgiving. Full employment will be maintained even if base wages and profit-sharing parameters are somewhat "too high" relative to aggregate demand or, equivalently, aggregate demand is "too low" relative to pay parameters.

Not all forms of share systems bring about equally desirable macroeconomic benefits. For example, such widely disparate systems as Employee Stock Ownership Plans and piece-rate formulas, unlike profit sharing, do not necessarily alter the employer's attitude about hiring or laying off workers.

Dealing with the Objections

Many of the objections that are traditionally raised against profit sharing involve a fallacy of composition: a fallacious generalization from what is ostensibly good for the tenured high-seniority insider worker, who already has job security, to the level of what is good for the community of all would-be workers, which is quite a different matter. Perhaps the worst example of this kind of fallacious compositional reasoning is the argument that profit sharing allegedly exposes workers to unnecessary risk.

This risk argument, so widely parroted and seemingly so plausible, embodies, at least in its crude form, a classical fallacy of composition. What is a correct statement for the individual high-seniority worker who already has job tenure is patently false for the aggregate of all would-be workers. The problem of unemployment is in fact the largest income risk that labor as a whole faces, as opposed to the median tenured worker, and it is concentrated entirely on the marginal or outsider worker. If more variable pay for the individual helps to preserve full employment for the group, while fixed pay for the individual tends to contribute to unemployment, it is not the least bit clear why overall welfare is improved by having the median worker paid a fixed wage. Actually, the correct presumption runs the other way around.

What is true for the individual tenured worker is not true for labor as a whole. When a more complete analysis is performed—one that considers the situation from the viewpoint of a neutral observer representing the entire population, rather than that of a tenured, high-seniority worker who already has job security—the welfare advantages of a profit-sharing system (which tends to deliver full employment) clearly outnumber those of a wage system (which permits unemployment). The basic reason is not difficult to understand. A wage system allows huge first-order losses of output and welfare to open up when a significant slice of the national income pie evaporates with unemployment. A profit-sharing system helps to stabilize aggregate output at the full employment level, creating the biggest possible national income pie, while permitting only small second-order losses to arise because of relatively limited random redistributions from a worker in one firm to a worker in another. It is extremely difficult to cook up an empirical real-world scenario, with reasonable numbers and specifications, in which a profit-sharing system with a moderate amount of profit sharing (say 20 percent of a worker's total pay) does not deliver significantly greater social welfare than a wage system does.

Any economy is full of uncertainty. There are no absolute guarantees, and if the uncertainty does not appear in one place, it will show up in another. It is much better, much healthier, if everyone shares some of that uncertainty at the beginning rather than letting it all fall on an unfortunate minority of employed workers who are drafted to serve as unpaid soldiers in the war against inflation. It is much fairer if people will agree that only 80 percent of their pay is going to be tied directly to the funny looking green pieces of paper—which are themselves an illusion, although a very useful one—and 20 percent will be tied to company profits per employee. Then the economy can be much more easily controlled to have full employment *and* stable prices. Society will be producing, and hence consuming, at its full potential. If people will face up to the uncertainty, and if everyone accepts some small part of it, society as a whole will end up with higher income and less uncertainty overall.

Another fallacy of composition often occurs when opponents of profit sharing argue that additional hired workers dilute the profits per worker that the previously hired workers receive, a factor that could cause the already existing labor force to resent newly hired workers and which, in extreme cases, might lead to restrictions against new hires. The fallacy of composition here lies in failing to account for the fact that widespread profit sharing and relatively free hiring would result in a tight labor market. Hence an employer could not so easily hire jobless people off the streets, because they are just not there.

Incidentally, this kind of profit-dilution argument is a red herring on other grounds as well. Even a one-sided worst-case scenario, where profit sharing "merely" dampens economic downturns by encouraging employers to lay off fewer workers during recessions, still represents a potentially enormous economic benefit to the community. If profit sharing did nothing more than reduce downside risks to an economy, it would still be tremendously important. In periods of recession and other kinds of squeeze, the "insiders" risk becoming "outsiders," and they may well be glad of a system which, without painful renegotiations, will enable an automatic adjustment in pay to be made—one that would be self-reversing in recovery—to preserve jobs. Remember, also, that even in periods of normal growth, there will always be firms under pressure to reduce employment; anything that lessens that pressure will help overall employment. To ratchet an economy toward a tight labor market and improve the employment-inflation tradeoff so that macroeconomic policies can be used more effectively requires only that, on the margin, a few less old workers are laid off during downswings and no fewer new workers are hired during upswings.

In comparing alternative payment mechanisms, remember the wage system is hardly ideal in terms of internal labor relations. Younger untenured workers are pitted against older high-seniority workers in the jobs vs. wages decision. Featherbedding is widespread. Workers resist the introduction of new labor-saving technology, resist job reassignments, and, more generally, take relatively little interest in the fortunes of the company because they do not have any direct stake in its profitability. Worker alienation is widespread in an environment where the employer is essentially indifferent on the margin to whether the worker stays or goes.

Arguments about profit sharing causing underinvestment are simply wrong, in theory and in practice. The critics have in mind a situation in which pay parameters are more or less permanently frozen. In that case, profit sharing would indeed cause under-investment for the well-publicized reason that any incremental profits would have to be shared with labor. (Incidentally, this fact should make workers pro-investment, so the critics cannot have it both ways in any case.) However, over the longer time horizon, one relevant to decisions about capital investments, both wage- and profit-sharing systems stimulate output equally; the marginal value of capital will equal the interest rate.

Even if this theoretical isomorphism between investment in wage and share systems, which is well understood in modern economic theory, did not exist, the cost of capital is only one side of the picture, probably the less important side. The more dominant consideration is the demand side. If profit sharing results in a macroeconomic environment in which output is being stabilized at or near the full-employment, full-capacity level, while a wage economy results in erratic, fluctuation-prone output and capacity utilization levels, there is bound to be more investment in a profit-sharing economy. And, as if these two arguments were not enough, interest rates, investment tax credits, and the like could be used to influence investment decisions in any system. The really important distinction concerns the average level of unemployed resources.

Joining the Issues

I began by commenting on some differences between the economist's and the industrial relations expert's views of labor payment systems and then proceeded to play the economist. I would like to return to that theme with a bit more emphasis on the industrial relations side, ending with a plea that we all move closer toward joining the issues because a lot of interesting and even important things may be at stake.

There are genuine, legitimate, tough issues involved in reconciling the many, already inherently conflictive, goals of traditional industrial relations with the additional burden of creating incentives to retain more workers during bad times and to hire more workers during good times. Any industrial relations system is a complicated package, of which pay is only one element. Trust between management and labor is an important part of most successful profit-sharing schemes. I do not pretend to know exactly how to design a socially optimal industrial relations pay system under the real-world constraints that exist. However, we should be placing much more emphasis on the employment consequences of industrial relations than we are now doing. In addition, anything resembling a socially optimal solution is very likely to involve some form of profit-related pay to help stabilize employment at higher levels. Government encouragement of widespread profit sharing, through moral persuasion and financial incentives, represents a decentralized, market-oriented way of improving national economic performance that is well worth pursuing.

References

Financial Times (March 20, 1986): 6.
Freeman, R., and M.L. Weitzman. "Bonuses and Employment in Japan." National Bureau of Economic Research Working Paper No. 1878, 1986.
Mitchell, D.J.B. "Gain Sharing: An Anti-Inflamatory Reform." *Challenge* 25 (July-August 1982): 18–25.
Weitzman, M.L. "Some Macroeconomic Implications of Alternative Compensation Systems." *Economic Journal* 93 (December 1983): 763–783.
———. *The Share Economy.* Cambridge, MA: Harvard University Press, 1984.
———. "The Simple Macroeconomics of Profit Sharing." *American Economic Review* 75 (1985): 937–953.
———. "Steady State Unemployment Under Profit Sharing." *Economic Journal* 97 (1987): 86–105.

9. NOTES ON GAIN SHARING

Robert J. Gordon

THE IDEA OF GAIN SHARING is not new. The age-old practice of piecework, the most common form of gain sharing, and "cost savings plans" (such as Improshare, the Scanlon Plan, and the Rucker Plan) long antedate the recent surge of interest in gain sharing, which is attributable in large part to Martin Weitzman's 1984 book, *The Share Economy*. What Weitzman has achieved already, irrespective of the validity of his claims, is twofold. He has redirected the participation and gain-sharing literature of labor economics toward an evaluation of macroeconomic consequences, as well as redirecting the macroeconomics literature toward employee compensation systems as a fundamental source of unemployment and stagflation.

The *New York Times* called Weitzman's proposal "the most important new idea in economics since Keynes," apparently intending this as a compliment (Passell, 1984). Interestingly, the flurry of attention devoted to Weitzman by macroeconomists has been notably one-sided. Hearing the word "Keynes," the best and brightest of the macroeconomists who think of themselves as neo-Keynesian jumped to attention and poured out symposia and conference discussion papers, while monetarists rolled over, yawned, and continued with their standard pastimes of attacking the Fed and pretending that the demand for money is not unstable after all.

The commentaries written since the publication of Weitzman's book include Cooper (1985), Mitchell (1985), Nordhaus (1985), Nordhaus and John (1986), and Summers (1986). In addition, conference discussions of the Weitzman plan and/or Weitzman papers have been presented by Alan Blinder, Robert Hall, and Robert Solow.

Alleged Implications of the Weitzman Proposal for Macroeconomics

The macroeconomic context for gain-sharing proposals is the evident failure of neo-Keynesian, monetarist, or new-classical

146

economists to provide a convincing recipe for perpetual prosperity. Developed economies have been racked with recurring business cycles since the dawn of the industrial revolution. The minimum achievable unemployment rate consistent with the avoidance of accelerating inflation (usually called the natural rate of unemployment or NAIRU) seems to have worsened over the past two decades in the U.S. and especially in Europe. Correspondingly, the Weitzman proposal predicts a decline in the amplitude in the business cycle of output and employment, as well as a decline in the NAIRU. These claims of a macroeconomic panacea resulting from revenue sharing clearly attract attention from those who are weary of making and/or listening to the same tired and mainly discredited solutions.

The two alleged achievements of dampening the business cycle and reducing the NAIRU are not, it should be stressed, the same thing. Economists since Keynes have recognized the role that rigid nominal wages play in aggravating the business cycle. Even before Weitzman, substantial attention was directed toward using wage flexibility as a means of achieving the relatively successful macroeconomic performance of Japan. Revenue sharing is only one of several possible ways of achieving greater wage flexibility and is unlikely to be the most desirable.

Thus it is the possibility of reducing the NAIRU that takes center stage, with its alluring promise of a macroeconomic free lunch in which output, employment, per-capita income, and government revenue permanently increase, while unemployment and the government deficit permanently decline. The promise of greater government revenue through higher income is essential in the Weitzman scheme. Firms and workers who for decades have resisted revenue sharing will have to be bribed with expensive tax subsidies to adopt revenue sharing, and the macroeconomic free lunch is Weitzman's crucial ingredient in arguing that the tax subsidies will not actually cost anything because they will be offset by added revenue.

Reducing NAIRU, however, hinges on the third and most controversial element of the Weitzman plan: the emergence of a perpetual *excess demand for labor* (set forth with the wonderful metaphor of "personnel office as a vacuum cleaner"). By turning the labor market upside down, converting it from a perpetual state of excess supply to one of excess demand, Weitzman's proposal has radical implications for the microeconomic aspects of labor relations. It raises fundamental questions about the economic motivations that have brought present U.S. institutional arrangements into being and the benefits and costs of trying to budge workers and firms loose from a compensation structure that they show no signs of voluntarily relinquishing.

This paper begins by examining the connection between gain sharing and the amplitude of business cycles and then turns to the microeconomic "vacuum cleaner" issues. It concludes with a brief examination of the connection between revenue sharing and the performance of the Japanese economy. Throughout, the primary emphasis is placed on revenue sharing rather than profit sharing, both in accordance with Weitzman's proposal and because profits are too small in relation to wage income to allow profit sharing to achieve a major change in the flexibility of wages.

Wage Flexibility, Employment Fluctuations, and Nominal GNP Indexation

If a complete revenue-sharing system were to be adopted and workers paid a fixed share of revenue, nominal wage payments per worker would automatically fall in response to a negative nominal demand shock affecting all firms. These demand shocks would be absorbed by the buffer of price changes, which firms could afford to make because their wage rates would be variable, and the demand shock would have little or no effect on output or employment. This system would behave much like a textbook classical economy. In addition to buffering employment from demand fluctuations, any occurrence of supply shocks (i.e., higher oil prices) would not create Keynesian unemployment because flexible wage rates in the non-oil sector of the economy would offset the influence of any boost in oil prices.

However, revenue sharing on a firm-by-firm basis is not unique in its ability to buffer the real economy from demand disturbances. Russell Cooper (1985) has made the related point that Weitzman's comparison of revenue sharing with a pure wage compensation scheme amounts to an attack on a straw man. Labor contract theorists have never latched onto a wage system as in any way privately or socially optimal, and their own derivations of optimal contracts always involve some form of adjustment of wage payments to contingencies. For example, if each firm were to pay workers a fixed fraction of its revenue, the nominal wage rate in the aggregate economy would act as if it were *indexed to nominal GNP*. The least controversial aspect of Weitzman's plan essentially involves nothing more than the statement that greater nominal wage flexibility—of which nominal GNP indexation is a limiting case—would stabilize output and employment.

Why is nominal GNP indexation superior to indexation of the

wage rate to the price level? Imagine that the growth rate of the nominal wage rate is initially set equal to the rate of inflation plus a constant ($w = p + a$), where a is the rate of productivity growth in some initial period. The growth rate of the real wage now becomes rigid at the rate a. Nominal GNP indexation automatically allows the growth rate of real wage rates to slow down in response to a productivity slowdown, such as that which occurred in the U.S. after 1973, whereas indexation to the price level does not. Nominal GNP indexation calls for the growth rate of nominal wages to slow down in tandem with nominal GNP growth, which after subtracting out inflation requires the growth rate of real wages to slow down in tandem with real GNP growth. At full employment, the growth rate of real GNP, and hence real wage rates, slows down in response to any slowdown in productivity growth.

Whether or not the rest of Weitzman's "share economy" package is adopted, nominal GNP indexation of the wage rate offers many advantages, leading one to ask why nominal GNP indexation has never been adopted by any known economy. The answer strikes at the heart of the risk that firms and workers accept when indexing to *anything*. Indexation to nominal GNP growth will be considered risky for workers in firms with a relatively stable demand (for example, services) because such a scheme would require them to take a wage cut that would be unnecessary under our present wage-contract economy.

But Weitzman's scheme entails analogous and inherently larger risks, because revenue sharing at the firm level requires that employees accept all the risk of their particular industry and their particular firm. Under revenue sharing, workers for Greyhound bus lines in 1981–85 would have suffered a severe cut in their standard of living in the wake of the invasion of People Express and other deregulated new airline entrants. Workers for People Express, in turn, would have suffered a decline in income of one-third in September 1986, as compared to September 1985, in a Weitzman economy. Smart workers, particularly those with enough seniority to be reasonably sure that they will not be laid off under the present wage system, would take a great risk in agreeing to index their wages to the revenue of a single vulnerable firm (even workers at such paragons as IBM and Bank of America must be feeling a bit uneasy these days). At a minimum, it is far more plausible for workers to risk tying their compensation to economy-wide aggregate revenue (i.e., nominal GNP) than to firm-specific revenue (the Weitzman scheme), and it is far more likely that they could be persuaded to do so (or, alternatively, the tax bribe needed to induce them would be smaller).

The Personnel Office as Vacuum Cleaner

Whatever the virtues of nominal GNP indexation of the wage rate, these are not the main emphases of Weitzman's case for the share-economy idea. Rather, his main argument lies in the fundamental change such an economy would cause in the balance of power between firms and workers. He vividly contrasts the showroom and the service departments of an automobile dealer: The eager salesmen, potted plants, and shiny floor of the showroom where the customer is king, versus the crabby foremen, poor lighting, and greasy floor of the service department where the worker is *not* king. He attributes the difference to the monopolistic element in auto pricing that sets price above marginal cost, in contrast to the conventional "wage economy" that sets a fixed wage for the service department worker, with marginal labor cost equal to average labor cost.

Weitzman implies that in a share economy, with marginal labor cost below average labor cost, the firm's enthusiasm about hiring new workers would result in foremen being sweet and reasonable, the service department being brightly lit, and the grease on the floor disappearing. All of these changes would occur because of a single "magic ingredient" in the share economy formula: The firm, through the simple act of hiring an additional worker, would induce existing workers to accept a wage cut.

The Central Role of Senior Workers

And here we come to the central issue: The entire benefit of the Weitzman scheme for the economy depends on an employment expansion to *reduce the wage rate of existing workers.* Does anyone involved in personnel administration believe that senior employees would agree to submit themselves to an unknown risk without contract restrictions and clauses that would undermine the social benefits of the Weitzman proposal? As their quid pro quo, workers will want to have some control over the level of employment and hence over the extent to which new employees will dilute the existing employees' share in firm revenue.

There are plenty of precedents for this. Salesmen negotiate exclusive territories, as do some managers of franchise stores. As a textbook author, I quiz prospective publishers mercilessly about the possibility that they might be planning to introduce a competitive book in my field. It is extremely likely that union workers, in particular, would press for contractual limits on the number of new hires. Seeing the relationship that exists between their own wage rates and the total number of employees under a revenue-sharing scheme, union workers might even demand that the firm reduce its existing employment level as normal attrition occurred.

The union aspect of revenue sharing has not received sufficient attention. (For an exception, see Mitchell, 1985, pp. 11–12.) Unions traditionally bargain with firms to increase their contractual wage rates. But under revenue sharing, an existing union worker can just as effectively raise his or her own wage rate by bargaining for contractual limits on the permissible increase in employment. In turn, any such limit not only reduces or eliminates the employment-expanding effect of the Weitzman plan, but also introduces microeconomic inefficiency by inhibiting dynamic firms that want to seize additional market share from making expansion plans that require extra employees.

Proponents of revenue sharing are tempted to weasel out of the difficulties caused by union bargaining either by pretending that unions do not exist or by pointing to the small share of union members in total U.S. employment. But nonunion workers are not powerless. If unions refused to adopt a compensation scheme that would threaten the standard of living of senior workers, unions might find nonunion workers much more willing to vote for union certification.

Any revenue-sharing plan inherently must create a conflict between the interests of senior workers and those who would be hired under the new system and who, under our present wage system, are unemployed. This conflict could easily erupt into open warfare. Efficient production in a particular plant often depends on cooperation among workers. Would such cooperation occur if senior workers had every incentive to make life for new hires so unpleasant that they would quit? Anything the senior workers could do without sacrificing firm revenue is a plausible outcome, including slashing tires in the parking lot and all the tricks that some established white residents in segregated communities have effected to victimize new and isolated minority residents. Would lawyers or professors engaged in recruiting activities to attract new junior associates try so hard when a dilution of their own salaries is at stake? I might be tempted to say, "Don't come to Northwestern in our economics department; you wouldn't be able to stand our winter climate!"

An important piece of evidence about the likely resistance of senior workers comes from the current operation of U.S. labor markets. The proliferation of two-tier wage systems in the airline and construction industries attests to the eagerness of firms to hire new workers by cutting wages but without the same reduction in the wage rate of senior workers called for under the Weitzman plan.

A Logical Loophole: Competitive Labor Markets for Senior Workers

In assessing the Weitzman proposal, a crucial distinction must be made between a competitive and noncompetitive labor market. In the simplest type of competitive labor market, all workers are identical and are paid the same wage. If workers have different skills, compensating wage differentials exactly match these differences in productivity. Competitive firms are indifferent among alternative workers, and they can always replace one worker with another by paying the "going" wage set by the market. Weitzman assumes precisely this competitive economy in his formal analysis, which includes the proposition that in long-run competitive equilibrium the share economy and wage economy are identical (Weitzman, 1983, proposition 1, p. 773).

Now imagine that we observe such a competitive economy with a wage system in place. Let workers be paid $80 per day, which is the wage rate given to the firm by supply and demand conditions in the economy as a whole. If the firm announces a cut in its wage rate from $80 to $60 per day for existing workers in order to maintain a fixed revenue share in the presence of newly hired additional workers, the existing workers will know that other $80 jobs are available in the competitive economy and will quit. Thus the claim that a switch to a share compensation system will push the marginal cost of labor below $80 in this competitive economy is logically flawed. By the very act of hiring additional workers, the firm would reduce the wage rate of the existing workers below $80 and they would quit. To avoid this mass exodus, the firm would *not* want to hire an additional worker starting from an initial $80 equilibrium situation. For any worker who could be hired at a lower wage, another one would quit, and there would in fact be no reduction in the effective marginal cost of labor (Nordhaus, 1985).

To salvage the share economy idea, we must account explicitly for noncompetitive aspects of the labor market. Training and mobility costs place a value on a "job match," and this value is shared by firms and workers in a proportion that may depend on bargaining. There may be potential for the firm to introduce a new compensation system that implies modest wage reductions for existing workers, yet maintains the wage rate above the next-best alternatives.

Does Weitzman Giveth to Employment What He Taketh From Investment?

In addition to creating strong incentives for intrafirm sabotage of younger workers by senior workers, the Weitzman scheme also creates adverse incentives for investment. By reducing capital's share of marginal revenue from 100 percent to a lesser percent, Weitzman must reduce the incentive for firms to invest. To the extent that the scheme provides an incentive for higher employment and lower investment, it must lead in the long run to a lower level of capital per worker and, hence, to a lower standard of living. The only escape from this logic is to claim that a higher level of overall employment in the economy will raise the number of employees per members of the population (and hence income per capita). Even this outcome is uncertain, however, because of the offsetting effects of increased employment and reduced investment.

The investment process also raises doubts about the alleged stimulus of the revenue-share economy to employment. Under the traditional wage compensation system, capital earns all of marginal revenue. Yet this does not lead to a permanent excess demand for capital, analogous to the permanent excess demand for labor that Weitzman claims would accompany a revenue-sharing system. Firms realize that adding extra units of capital would reduce the earnings of old units of capital, and so they resist such an expansion, just as senior workers would resist the employment expansion claimed to occur under revenue sharing.

The Case of Japan

Weitzman has pointed to the Japanese bonus system as a possible cause for the outstanding performance of the Japanese economy, including rapid growth, low unemployment, and low inflation. However, Nordhaus and John (1986) have shown that Japanese bonus payments do not vary enough from year to year to qualify as a disguised profit-sharing system.

Also, an anonymously written paper that I recently refereed concluded that the bonus system increased the elasticity of

Japanese labor-compensation payments to nominal demand by only about 5 percent. The latter set of results suggests that the performance of Japan depends more on the cyclical flexibility of the *base wage* than on any extra flexibility added by the bonus payment.

Further, the much-discussed Japanese attributes of participation and teamwork contrast with the sabotage of new workers by senior workers that would be likely (at least if incentives mean anything) under a share economy. In my 1982 paper (Gordon, 1982), I pointed to the role of wage stickiness in aggravating U.S. business fluctuations and to the role of flexible wages in dampening Japanese fluctuations, but I cannot find any evidence that the key ingredient in Japan is revenue sharing. More important is the simultaneous expiration of one-year contracts, so that labor contracts on a national basis can emulate a system of nominal GNP indexation without exposing any particular set of employees to the risk of the misfortune of a single firm that is inherent in revenue sharing and would surely undermine its appeal to any rational set of senior workers. The anecdotal evidence of successful profit sharing by the Worthington, Steelcase, and Michigan Steel companies in Leib (1986) is the exception that proves the rule, because all these companies are nonunion and at least the first two have profits that are more stable than average.

Conclusion

My sharp critique of gain sharing in this paper should not be taken to represent outright opposition to any new form of compensation. Any reform which moves in the direction of nominal GNP indexation would have my full support.

References

Cooper, R. "Sharing Some Thoughts on Weitzman's *The Share Economy.*" National Bureau of Economic Research Working Paper No. 1734, October 1985.

Gordon, R.J. "Why U.S. Wage and Employment Behavior Differs from That in Britain and Japan." *Economic Journal* 92 (1982): 13–44.

Leib, J.A. "The Promise in Profit Sharing." *New York Times* (February 9, 1986): 10.

Mitchell, D. "The Share Economy and Industrial Relations: Implications of the Weitzman Proposal." U.C.L.A. Institute of Industrial Relations Working Paper No. 99, November 1985.

Nordhaus, W.D. "Can the Share Economy Conquer Stagflation?" Yale Working Paper, April 1985.

Nordhaus, W.D., and A. John, eds. "The Share Economy: A Symposium."
   Cowles Foundation Discussion Paper No. 783, February 1986.
Passell, P. "The Hidden Boon in Profit-Sharing." *New York Times*
   (November 15, 1984): 30.
Weitzman, M.L. "Some Macroeconomic Implications of Alternative
   Compensation Systems." *The Economic Journal* 93 (December 1983):
   763–83.
———. *The Share Economy*. Cambridge, MA: Harvard University Press,
   1984.

10. The Promise of Gain Sharing*

Robert B. McKersie

WE AGAIN APPEAR TO BE in a period of social history when considerable interest is being shown in the concept of gain sharing. There are various definitions; the language used by the Profit Sharing Research Foundation captures some of the key elements:

> A system incentive (or gain-sharing plan) motivates the individual as an individual and as a member of a productive team. It is a participation incentive and increases productivity as a result of employee cooperation and involvement.

In some early work that George Shultz and I did on this subject, we used the trilogy of participation, achievement, and rewards to capture the key features of what have come to be called gain-sharing plans.

The "participation" premise of gain sharing rests on the assumption that all members of the organization, if given an opportunity, can solve problems and make a contribution beyond what might be thought of as standard performance. As a result of emphasizing team work and coordination across all elements of the business unit, costs can be reduced, products delivered on schedule, quality improved, and a host of other important achievements realized that favorably affect the bottom line.

The "achievement" part of the program places emphasis on reducing costs and increasing profits in distinction to the emphasis of piece work and other individual incentive systems on improving productivity by inducing workers to produce more units in a given period of time. As the phrase goes, the big gains come from "working smarter, not harder"—this is the essence of the achievement that is sought via gain sharing.

Rewards are paid at intervals, sometimes monthly or quarterly, sometimes in cash and in other instances deferred into pension

*Reprinted with permission from *ILR Reports* Vol. XXIV, No. 1, Fall 1986, Published by the New York State School of Industrial and Labor Relations, Cornell University, Ithaca, New York. Copyright 1986 by Cornell University.

programs. A distinguishing feature is that all members of the
business unit receive a payout (usually figured as a percentage of
their base pay); the plan thereby focuses on the performance of the
unit as the achieving team.

A Field Guide to the Species

When the term gain sharing is mentioned, many branded products
are available and there are even some unbranded or generic
varieties on the scene. In classifying the schemes that are being
used, I find it useful to distinguish between those that are
motivational versus those that have organizational equity as their
purpose.

The motivational category includes such plans as Scanlon,
Rucker, and Improshare. In terms of the concepts of participation,
achievement, and rewards, these plans identify the participating
group as those employees at a particular location such as a store, a
factory, or an office; the achievement emphasis is on reducing costs,
primarily the labor factor; and rewards are paid usually on a
monthly basis.

By contrast, organizational equity plans seek to reward the
organization for gains that have accrued on a global basis. Thus,
profit sharing, which usually pays the same percentage to all
members of the organization (across all facilities and locations), is a
simple and clear method of "sharing the fruits." But unless the plan
applies to subunits, that is, to natural achieving components, profit
sharing is likely to be seen as a fringe benefit without much
motivational value.

While the term gain sharing thus describes a range of approaches,
most of the discussion in this article will consider Scanlon, Rucker,
Improshare, and their generic descendents.

Reasons for the Surge of Interest

While there are no firm statistics, rough estimates are that there are
over 1000 plans in the motivational category and many more in the
organizational equity category. And these numbers are growing
rapidly.

Here at MIT where the Scanlon Plan was designed and first
introduced, a conference organized by Fred Lesieur and Associates
is held every other year and brings together representatives, both
management and labor, from sites that have the plan as well as those

that are investigating its possibility. Interest has remained at a high level and this past fall we held the twenty-first gathering, with several hundred participants in attendance. Carl Frost and Associates hold conferences for Scanlon companies and unions in their orbit (mainly in the Midwest) and attendance at these events has increased dramatically.

More evidence of the surge of interest can be seen in the fact that half of the sites that we are currently studying for the U.S. Department of Labor to determine the staying power of different types of innovations in industrial relations are considering some type of gain sharing. (It should be noted that our choice of these sites did not involve the subject of gain sharing. Rather we chose these sites because of the experimentation that was taking place with quality of work life, labor management committees dealing with training, and union representation on the board. As a number of these sites have moved further into the transformation process, they have turned their attention to some type of gain sharing.)

One of the most significant indications of the fact that gain sharing appears to be at the top of the agenda for many companies (and unions) is that it represents a key provision in the design of the new Saturn plant. Specifically, the agreement between General Motors and the UAW provides for the development of some type of gain-sharing plan that will allow the workers at the new plant to move from their base pay, set at 80 percent of the industry wage rate, to higher levels—presumably to 100 percent and above.

What explains the surge of interest in gain sharing? Some of the increased activity stems from the very pragmatic consideration that workers, who have given up concessions in the form of wage cuts and reduced fringe benefits, require some quid pro quo if these concession agreements are to be salable.

There is also considerable interest these days, especially on the part of management, in making compensation much more flexible. A gain sharing plan does just this—it only pays out a bonus when economic performance is better. In fact a whole movement has developed, spearheaded by the work of Martin Weitzman and his key book, *The Share Economy,* that presents a well-thought-through theoretical argument about the overall advantage in having wages be more flexible and tied to the performance of the firm.

Finally, in many situations gain sharing is being introduced as "the frosting on the cake." Over the past several years many companies have introduced new work systems that emphasize the use of teams, problem solving, and delegation of management to operating personnel—with remarkably positive results. When these "high commitment" systems produce better than average economic results, management often finds it desirable to engage in some sharing of these gains—both from an equity point of view and as a way of institutionalizing the changes and motivating the organization to continue the process of improving economic performance.

The Relationship of Gain Sharing to the Employee Involvement Movement

The preceding comments suggest that in a number of situations today gain sharing is being introduced as a final piece that locks in place a new system of work organization and involvement. This is an extremely important point and some elaboration is in order. It is interesting to contrast the circumstances that led to the use of gain sharing for most of the post–World War II period and those that obtain today for situations where gain sharing is coming on the scene for the first time.

To take the Scanlon Plan as a case in point, most of the early installations occurred where the Scanlon Plan represented a solution to some type of crisis or severe economic problem. In a good number of cases the firm was bankrupt or about to go under. In other situations traditional incentives of the individual and small group variety had become dysfuntional; rather than take the "pull" of an incentive out of the situation altogether, the parties had replaced piece work with the Scanlon Plan. And then in a few instances the introduction of the Scanlon Plan came about as a result of a philosophical commitment by management to involve workers and to share the economic gains. Often this value commitment to the principles of gain sharing occurred where the businesses were privately held and the owners wanted to foster a family-type culture.

In passing, it should be noted that early gain sharing, especially the Scanlon formulation, was seen by scholars and other commentators as one of the best examples of progressive labor-management relations. Douglas MacGregor and his famous Theory Y (the book was published twenty-five years ago) gave prominent attention to the Scanlon Plan as a device for achieving positive labor relations. Students in industrial relations courses knew about the Scanlon Plan because it captured the imagination of analysts who hoped that labor-management relations would be more than just an adversary system that distributed the profits accompanying a growing economy. While it was not described as the "new industrial relations," nevertheless gain sharing possessed many features of what has come to be known today as the new or non-traditional system of labor-management relations.

Just why gain sharing did not diffuse more than it did between the 1940s and the late 1970s is not clear. It captured the participation elements that are so central to the quality of work life movement today; it decentralized responsibility to lower levels of the organization in the same way that characterizes current efforts to eliminate levels of management and to push responsibility downward; and it created much more flexibility in compensation and in the deployment of labor—again, themes that are preeminent today. The answer is not completely clear.

Some of the reasons for this absence of widespread diffusion may be related to some inherent limitations of gain sharing which I will touch on later. But for the most part the explanation for the limited role of gain sharing until recently must rest with factors of tradition, the absence of a crisis, and management's desire to keep control and to keep workers and their union representatives within traditional boundaries.

Nevertheless, today gain sharing appears to be an idea (perhaps an old one) whose time has come. Today, it does not come to the scene as a brand new idea but as part of a larger system of concepts; in this respect it is not by itself carrying the full load of introducing participation, delegation of responsibility, and the restructuring of compensation toward more flexible forms.

In some respects the use of financial incentives in industry has come full circle. As of 1960, when Slichter, Healy, and Livernash wrote their classic book entitled *The Impact of Collective Bargaining on Management,* wage payment systems that related extra pay to extra performance covered approximately 30 percent of the production and maintenance workers in the United States. That coverage has dropped steadily as management abandoned these traditional incentives in favor of measured day work and salary plans. By getting rid of variable pay, management was able to establish control over worker effort and to allow technology and performance-monitoring systems to elicit acceptable levels of worker effort.

Now financial incentives are returning, although they emphasize targets for improving economic performance other than increased output and they are being applied to large units of the corporation.

The Benefits of Gain Sharing

A much-cited study by the General Accounting Office estimates that the introduction of some form of gain sharing on average increases productivity by 17 percent. This has a sizable impact on profits. Other gains from the viewpoint of the organization include: economic education (a process that is inherent in spelling out problems for the organization), improved team work between all groups in the organization (especially between office and factory personnel), management development (companies have often spotted talent in the screening and suggestion committees), increased flexibility in the use of labor (workers spend considerably less time worrying about job jurisdictions) and the acceptance of change. From an institutional point of view, labor-management relations usually are improved; it is hard to separate cause and effect, however, because labor-management relations need to be positive before a gain-sharing plan can be installed. For a recent case study that documents the range of improvements that can accompany gain sharing (and employee involvement), see the U.S. DOL publication on Eggers Industries.

From the workers' side of the ledger, aside from higher earnings (the payouts usually average about 10 percent), there are other gains such as fewer health problems and more job satisfaction. The latter findings were noted by James Driscoll in a comparison of Scanlon sites with a matched set of sites not using any form of gain sharing.

Factors That Help a Gain-Sharing Plan Work

Organizations have found that a gain-sharing plan does not run itself. Management must develop a plan to keep the program energized. This means spelling out problems and communicating on an open and full basis about areas that need attention or about developments that present challenges to the organization, for example, the introduction of new technology.

Management must give up tight control and be willing to listen to the suggestions that are stimulated by the plan and to defer judgment on the best course of action until the organization has had a chance to grapple with the problems at hand.

Gain-sharing systems only work when a structure is in place that enables all members of the organization to participate, to come forward with ideas, and to have these ideas discussed and evaluated as well as reviewed and authorized by the proper personnel. All of the skills that are involved in making quality of work life programs and labor-management committees effective are central for making a gain-sharing plan effective.

Another factor that is essential for making a gain-sharing plan effective is the provision of some type of assurance that members of the organization will not become unemployed as the result of the plan's operating successfully. When gain-sharing plans first came on the scene in the late 1940s, the provision of this type of employment security assurance was difficult for firms to institute, primarily because the technical know-how was not present to implement such a commitment. Today, more and more organizations realize that they can manage attrition and work flows so that the consequences of decisions that are within the control of the organization (such as displacement due to new technology or in this case the improvement of productivity as a result of a gain-sharing plan) will not redound to the detriment of the organization. Precisely because of human resource planning and the knowledge of ways in which to accelerate attrition if excess people are on hand, it is much more feasible today than in an earlier era for management to give employment assurances.

These precepts regarding what it takes to make a plan successful were supported in a survey that Joel Cutcher-Gershenfeld conducted at our 1985 Scanlon Conference. When the participants were asked to rank the driving forces for successful operation, the following factors received 75 percent of the votes:

16% Management support
14% Employee involvement
12% Good communications
 9% Trust
 6% Change in labor-management attitudes
 5% Union cooperation
 5% Willingness to listen
 4% Appropriate financial rewards
 4% Immediate implementation of ideas

Problems and Challenges

Obviously, since gain sharing (even with the rapid growth now taking place) has not diffused to more than a small fraction of employment (the high-side estimate would be 20 percent of all employees), substantial problems must exist and they involve more than the assertion that "management does not know a good thing when it sees it." At this point it is necessary to touch on some of the inherent difficulties or limitations of gain-sharing plans; the next section considers some of the steps being taken to deal with some of these issues.

First, a number of organizations have found a type of plateau effect with the installation of gain sharing, that is, dramatic results occurring over the first several years but then stagnation instead of continuing improvement. Scanlon Plans typically arrive at the employee bonus by computing the ratio of labor costs to sales and then comparing this ratio to a similar ratio from the past. One of the reasons for the leveling off of results is that most gain sharing plans find it hard to adjust the payoff when conditions change. If product or technology changes lead to cost reduction, then the payment of bonuses based on improvement in performance compared to a historical period may distribute rewards that are not justified. On this score profit sharing possesses a distinct advantage, if the plan is designed so that it only pays a bonus when the performance of the corporation is better than some market average.

Given the fact that many companies feel that their compensation costs are already above market, these same companies may be leery of entering into a system that would generate bonuses, even though large monetary concessions may have been instituted in the same negotiations that provided for a gain-sharing plan. The point is that costs may have to be driven down so substantially and so rapidly—with management taking the initiative (the organization cannot be expected to initiate such dramatic changes)—that it is not feasible for the company to share even a portion of these gains with employees. And other companies do not want to experience the uncertainty of whether they will be able to revise the ratio when circumstances change.

Another challenge of gain sharing, mentioned earlier, is that it requires a continuing effort to maintain its vitality and the commitment of the organization to its operation. Some companies that have used the approach have found a type of generational sequence wherein the plan works for a period of time (sometimes as long as ten to twelve years) and then starts to lose its momentum because the organization has not been successful in orienting new members. This type of life cycle (identified by Lawrence Williams in some early work on gain sharing) is probably inevitable and suggests some type of periodic refurbishing operation that refocuses the attention of the organization on the basics of the plan.

Another problem, one quite pertinent to the current scene, is that a gain-sharing plan can be negotiated and ratified with exaggerated expectations that it will provide an opportunity for the workers to recoup their concessions. If a plan is installed on such a basis, then it is not a plan that will last long, because it will be a disappointment for employees and create problems for management. Gain sharing requires that there be new gains before there can be sharing.

Space does not permit a full discussion of all issues and challenges that are involved in the effective implementation of a gain-sharing plan. The following list, taken from the Cutcher-Gershenfeld survey, ranks the factors that received 75 percent of the votes for barriers in the operation of a Scanlon Plan:

- 12% Improper follow-up
- 10% Unwillingness to adapt to change and fear of the unknown
- 9% Lack of trust
- 6% Lack of knowledge of the plan (it is complex) at all levels—leading to mistrust
- 6% Unwillingness of some managers to allow time for participation
- 6% Negative peer pressure
- 5% Unwillingness of management and labor to give up traditional roles
- 5% Lack of communication
- 5% Lack of funds to implement suggestions
- 4% First-line supervisors' fear of losing authority
- 4% Employees' fear of job loss from suggestions
- 4% Focusing only on financial aspects of the plan and forgetting the participative part

New Perspectives on the Design of Gain-Sharing

Given the inherent weakness of gain sharing in that the ratio against which bonuses are determined is not adjusted over time to accurately measure achievement, some new thinking is required to keep gain sharing in step with current economic realities. One possibility is to base the ratio on external or competitive standards, for example the price at which a particular operation can be purchased on the outside, should management decide to "stop the 'make' and shift to the 'buy'."

To the extent that profits can be measured for the business unit, then they can be figured into the standards against which true performance can be measured. Historically, the difficulty with profit sharing has been that it used only one bench mark, the overall performance of the company. With profit information available on a more decentralized basis and with companies more willing to reveal such information, it may be possible to use these measures in the design of gain sharing.

Another idea relates to the fact that payment under a gain-sharing plan does not necessarily have to derive from a formula, that is, payment of certain bonus levels for certain levels of achievement on an ongoing basis. Often, true achievement is an episodic event and organizations might consider paying one-shot rewards for such achievement. For example, one of the airlines that we have been studying gained a windfall in business several years ago when a competitor went on strike. The resulting challenge for the work force was to perform so effectively that the customers who were shifted by the strike would choose to continue to fly with the replacement airline. In cases such as this it should be possible to identify what would be considered extra achievement and then to pay some special bonus to the organization. It would not make sense to pay this bonus on a continuing basis but only for the extra effort and extra service that were required during the opportunity period afforded by the strike.

Time and time again organizations that are involved in high commitment systems have said in effect, "We would like to find a way to recognize impressive economic results but we do not want to enter into a formal gain-sharing plan that would get us tied up in a system that might be hard to revise in the future." The answer is to fashion a variety of ad hoc economic rewards that share the benefits of higher performance and reinforce a high commitment system.

The Future of Gain Sharing

We are at a point where, for reasons outlined above, there is considerable interest in this concept. For organizations that are able to set up new operations and to introduce all of the principles of the new industrial relations, gain sharing can be a key feature, albeit only a piece of a larger system.

For most organizations that are locked up in traditions and status quo arrangements, on the other hand, gain sharing can be a powerful intervention for more general organizational change. For one thing, it signals to everyone in the organization the importance of improving economic performance. By contrast, quality of work life is usually introduced on a voluntary basis and our experience is that it never applies to more than 40 or 50 percent of the organization.

Clearly, the wage payment dimension (that is, sharing rewards) of gain sharing is a powerful technique for getting the attention of the organization. The test is to design the plan and to administer the plan in a way that induces the business unit to strive for better results and to share rewards that represent true achievement on a continuing basis. Surely, the parties with an interest in today's employment relationships should be able to think creatively about the opportunity and the challenge of designing and implementing viable gain-sharing plans.

References

Driscoll, J.W. "A Multiple-Consistency, Control-Group Evaluation of the Scanlon Plan." Sloan School of Management Working Paper, 1982.
"Employee Involvement and Gain Sharing Produce Dramatic Results at Eggers Industries." U.S. DOL Bureau of Labor-Management Relations and Cooperative Programs, March 1985.
Kochan, T.A.; H.C. Katz; and R.B. McKersie. *The Transformation of American Industrial Relations.* New York: Basic Books, 1986.
Productivity Sharing Programs, Report of the Government Accounting Office, U.S. Congress, March 1981.
Schultz, G., and R. McKersie. "Participation-Achievement-Reward Systems." *Journal of Management Studies* 10 (May 1973): 141–161.

NOTES ON CONTRIBUTORS

ALLEN CHEADLE performs economic analysis in health policy at the University of Washington.

GRANT M. DAVIS is Distinguished Professor of Business Administration at the University of Arkansas.

ROBERT J. GORDON is the Stanley G. Harris Professor of Economics at Northwestern University.

PATRICK G. GRASSO and **TERRY J. HANFORD** are employed by the Program Evaluation and Methodology Division of the U. S. General Accounting Office.

W. BRUCE JOHNSON is professor of accounting at the school of business at the University of Iowa.

ROBERT C. McKERSIE is professor of industrial relations at the Sloan School of Management, Massachusetts Institute of Technology.

GEORGE T. MILKOVICH is professor of industrial and labor relations at the New York State School of Industrial and Labor Relations at Cornell University.

MYRON J. ROOMKIN is professor of human resources management at the J. L. Kellogg Graduate School of Management of Northwestern University.

RAYMOND RUSSELL teaches sociology at the University of California at Riverside.

GEORGE STRAUSS is professor of business administration at the University of California, Berkeley.

NORMAN A. WEINTRAUB is Chief Economist of the International Brotherhood of Teamsters, Chauffeurs, Warehousemen, and Helpers of America.

MARTIN C. WEITZMAN is the Mitsui Professor of Economics at the Massachusetts Institute of Technology.

JOHN L. ZALUSKY is an economist with the American Federation of Labor-Congress of Industrial Organization in Washington, D. C.

INDEX

Adler, M. J.   80, 98
Akerloff, G. A.   20
Antle, R.   130

Balderston, C. C.   48
Benston, G. J.   126, 128
Bhagat, S.   129, 132
Blasi, J.   35
Blinder, A.   146
Bloom, S. M.   87
Bokovoy, P.   11
Bowers, D. G.   3
Brandes, S.   52
Brickley, J.   129, 132
Broderick, R. F.   109
Brone, R.   70
Brubaker, O.   68
Bullock, R. J.   110, 113
Buyouts   12–14

Cable, J.   36
Campbell, J. P.   111
Carlson, N. W.   22
Cheadle, A.   x, 11, 20, 25, 28, 30, 62
Chelius, J.   vii
Coburn, C. L.   69
Coch, L.   3
Cohen, A.   87
Cole, R.   18
Conte, M.   35, 46, 87
Cook, H.   35, 87
Cooper, R.   146, 148
Coughlan, A.   126, 130
Cutcher-Gershenfeld, J.   162, 164

Davis, G.   x–xi
Doyle, R. J.   110
Driscoll, J.   12, 161
Dyer, L.   114, 115, 116

Ehrenberg, R. G.   111, 131
Estrin, S.   32

Finseth, E.   31
Fitzroy, F.   36
Ford, R. N.   3
Foulkes, F. K.   116
Fox, H.   123
Frazer, D.   11
French, J. R. P.   3
Frost, C. F.   16, 112, 158
Future   55–57, 77, 95, 107–108, 165–66

Gain Sharing, types of   21–36, 98, 157
Gompers, S.   66–67
Goodman, P.   3
Gordon, R. J.   xii, 154
Gould, R.   11
Granrose, C. S.   98
Grasso, P.   xi
Green, W.   67–68, 71
Griffin, R.   18
Grossman, S.   125
Guest, R.   3

Hackman, R. J.   3, 15
Hall, R.   146
Hammer, R. H.   11, 14, 35, 111
Hanford, T. J.   xi
Harris, D.   124
Harris, M.   124, 125, 129, 130
Hart, O.   125
Healy, P.   128
Heller   16
Hetter, P.   80

Hewitt Associates   26–27, 28, 77
History   2–3, 66–71, 79–81, 97, 109, 160
Hite, G.   124
Holder, G. W.   114, 115, 116
Holmstrom, B.   125
Human resource practices   114–120, 131–32, 133, 138–39, 145, 161–62

Improshare   23–24, 109, 113, 146, 157
Ivancic, C.   85

Jachim, T. C.   98
Jackall, R.   14
Jacoby, S. M.   9
Japan   138–39, 153–54
Job redesign   3, 4, 6, 17
John, A.   146–153
Johnson, B.   xi–xii, 125, 129, 130
Johnson, G. E.   75
Jones, D.   36

Kang, S.   128
Katz, H. C.   9, 15, 17, 114
Kelso, L.   80–81, 82, 83, 94, 98
Kelso, P.   80
Keynes, J. M.   146–47, 148
Klein, J.   15
Klein, K.   12, 35, 36, 81, 84, 87
Kochan, T. A.   9, 15, 17, 114
Kruse, D.   30, 31, 35, 36

Lambert, R.   126, 128, 129
Langdon, J. N.   2
Larcker, D.   112, 125, 127, 128, 129
Lawler, E.   3, 12, 38, 40, 110, 113, 114, 131
Lazear, E.   125–27
Lease, R.   129, 132
Leib, J. A.   70
Lesieur, F. G.   110, 112, 157
Levin, H. M.   14

Levine, D.   32
Lewellen, W.   128
Lewin, K.   2
Lewis, J. L.   68, 110
Likert, R.   2, 114
Locke, E.   5
Loderer, C.   128
Lohmann, J.   35, 87
Long, M.   124, 128
Long, R.   46, 81
Lowin, A.   5

MacGregor, D.   159
Macy, B.   3
Magee, R.   129, 130
Marrow, A. J.   3
Marsh, T. R.   35, 87
McAllister, D. E.   35, 87
McGregory, D.   114
McKersie, R. B.   xii, 20, 110, 114, 156
Metzger, B. L.   iii, xii–xiii, 30, 46, 47, 110
Milkovich, G. T.   xi, xii, 111, 112, 117, 131
Miller, J. J.   98
Miller, M.   124
Mitchell, D. J. B.   47, 109, 146, 151
Montgomery, R. E.   74
Mowrer, N.   9, 15, 17
Murphy, K.   112, 126, 127

Newman, J.   117
Nordhaus, W. D.   146, 152, 153
Norton, L.   3
Nuti, D. M.   57

O'Dell, C. S.   109, 110
Olson, D. G.   98

Palepu, K.   128
Parker, M.   16
Participation, types of   6–14, 84–86

Passell, P.   146
Perry, S.   14
Peterson, M.   3
Piore, M.   4
Pritchard, R. B.   111
Problems   15–18, 76–77, 31–32, 110, 133–34, 142–45, 150–52,
     162–65
Proctor, P.   99
Profit Sharing Council   26–27
Profit Sharing Research Foundation   25, 29

Quality circles   3, 4, 8–10, 12, 17–18
Quarrey, M.   35, 36, 87, 132

Raviv, A.   125
Rhodes, S.   46
Rosen, C.   12, 35, 36, 81, 84, 85, 87
Rosen, S.   124, 125
Rosenfeld, A.   128
Ross, J.   5
Roth, R.   74
Rothschild-Whitt, J.   34
Rucker Plan   23–24, 113, 146, 157
Ruh, R. A.   16, 112
Russell, R.   xi, 14

Sable, C.   4
Sayles, L.   15
Scanlon, J. N.   68, 112
Scanlon Plan   12, 23–24, 109, 112, 113, 146, 157, 158, 159–160,
     161, 162–63, 164
Schmidt, R.   126, 130
Scholes, M.   124
Schuster, M. H.   12, 113
Schweiger, D. M.   5
Seashore, S. E.   3
Shaw, L.   74, 76
Shaw, W.   66
Shultz, G.   110, 156
Smith, A.   130

Solow, R.   146
Spence, M.   125
Staw, B.   5
Steers, J.   20, 46
Stelzer, I. M.   74
Stern, R.   11, 14, 35, 46
Strauss, G.   ix–x, 11, 12, 15

Tannenbaum, A.   35, 36, 46, 87
Tehranian, H.   128, 129
Theory   5, 19–21, 74–76, 111–12, 123–26, 140, 146–48
Tove, T.   46
Trachman, M.   35, 87
Travlos, N.   128

Wachter, M.   124
Waegelein, J.   128, 129
Wagner, I.   35, 87
Walking, R.   128
Wallace, R. L.   112
Walton, R. E.   15, 18, 114
Weintraub, N.   x–xi
Weitzman, M. C.   xii, 20, 30, 46, 74, 80, 146, 147, 148, 149, 150,
    151, 152, 153, 158
Whyte, W. F.   13, 98
Williams, L.   163
Williamson, O.   124
Wolfson, M.   128
Wyatt, S.   2

Yellen, J.   124
Young, K.   12, 36, 81, 84

Zalusky, J.   x